THE BEST PITTSBURGH SPORTS ARGUMENTS

THE 100 MOST CONTROVERSIAL, DEBATABLE QUESTIONS FOR DIE-HARD FANS

JOHN MEHNO

SOURCEBOOKS, INC.®
NAPERVILLE, ILLINOIS

Published by Sourcebooks, Inc.
P.O. Box 4410, Naperville, Illinois 60567-4410
(630) 961-3900
Fax: (630) 961-2168
www.sourcebooks.com

Library of Congress Cataloging-in-Publication Data

Mehno, John.
  The best Pittsburgh sports arguments : the 100 most controversial,
debatable questions for die-hard fans / John Mehno.
     p. cm.
  Includes index.
  ISBN-13: 978-1-4022-0967-3 (pbk.)
  ISBN-10: 1-4022-0967-3 (pbk.)
  1. Sports—Pennsylvania—Pittsburgh—Miscellanea. 2. Athletes—
Pennsylvania—Pittsburgh—Miscellanea. 3. Sports teams—
Pennsylvania—Pittsburgh—Miscellanea. I. Title.

GV584.5.P57M45 2007
796.'0974886—dc22

                                    2007028606

                Printed and bound in the United States of America.
                     CH 10 9 8 7 6 5 4 3 2 1

For Hoover and Franny

CONTENTS

Penguins Points

Pittsburgh Places

On the Air

Arts and Letters

Pittsburgh People

Hits and Misses

INTRODUCTION

Being a Pittsburgh sports fan is a lifelong commitment. It starts when Mom and Dad proudly wrap the baby in that first Terrible Towel and it may end the way it did for James Henry Smith.

When James died of prostate cancer at age 55 in 2005, his family wanted to give him an appropriate farewell. A cooperative funeral director arranged to have his viewing in a setting that would symbolize his devotion to the Steelers. So James's body was dressed in black and gold silk pajamas, covered with a Steelers-logo lap blanket, and placed in a recliner with a remote in his hand and beer and cigarettes at his side. A high-definition TV set played a continuous loop of Steelers highlights.

In many locales, news coverage of that story would be greeted by raised eyebrows. In Pittsburgh, a lot of men nodded and thought, "You know, that's a hell of an idea."

Every city loves its teams, but few have the passion for sports that Pittsburgh does. How many weekends revolve around football, starting with a high school game on Friday night and wrapping up with the Steelers on Sunday afternoon? Not many individuals in the United States watch hockey on television, but TV ratings for the Penguins are through the roof in Pittsburgh. The Pirates have gone more than a decade without a winning season, a streak of futility that inspires anger rather than apathy in Pittsburgh. Bad as it's been, fans still care.

People who have no patience in a supermarket line will hold the phone line for a half hour to get on a talk show and complain for 30 seconds about the Steelers' special teams. Pittsburgh tough guys are brought to tears on only two occasions: when their daughters marry, and when NFL Films shows those misty slow-motion films of Jack Lambert destroying a quarterback. By the way, it's okay to wear a Steelers jacket to a wedding in Pittsburgh—even if you're the groom.

When the steel industry collapsed in the 1970s and times were tough, Sunday afternoons offered redemption. Steel may have betrayed Pittsburgh, but the Steelers were still there, beating up Cleveland and exacting revenge for all those tough seasons in the 1960s. Pittsburgh is a place where priests working noon masses keep the sermons short because they know there's a one o'clock kickoff—and most of them are anxious to see the game, too. Pittsburgh fans hold some truths dear: The Oakland Raiders are forever evil, NHL referees have it in for the Penguins, and network commentators *never* give Pittsburgh teams enough credit.

TV meteorologists don't know whether to call subzero wind chills frigid or polar; sports fans know that's simply

Steelers weather. It isn't always easy being a fan. Prices are always going up, new venues wreck tailgating traditions, the Pirates test everyone's patience. But no one ever really drops out. It's in the blood, and it transcends zip codes. There are bars where Steelers fans gather on Sundays across the country.

This book is for everyone who peeked around a pole at Forbes Field to see big Bob Veale fire a fastball, for everyone who climbed that hill in Oakland to sit in the rain and watch the Steelers or the Panthers at Pitt Stadium. It's for those who felt wistful when Three Rivers Stadium was blown up, and those who wish the Pirates were as fabulous as the panorama at PNC Park. It's for those who laughed at Max Korfendigas's tipsy golf tips on Rege Cordic's radio show ("birdies and eagles, Rege, anything with feathers is good") and those who laugh at Scott Paulsen's "spit, choke 'n' puke" sportscasts.

It's for the people who buy 50-50 raffle tickets at high school games, for everyone who ever taped one of Myron Cope's Steelers Christmas songs, and for anyone who cheered along with Mossie Murphy at Duquesne or Tiger Paul at Pitt. It's for the kids who stole Bob Prince's "Kiss it goodbye" when they hit a wiffle ball home run, and for the ones who borrow Mike Lange's "he shoots and scores" in street hockey.

This book covers a lot of years and a lot of ground— everything from whether Neil O'Donnell really single-handedly lost Super Bowl XXX to which Steelers' fight song rocks more. There's a lot to discuss, and it's certain you have some strong opinions. You're a Pittsburgh fan, after all. Thanks for reading, and enjoy the debate.

HERE WE GO, STEELERS

WHAT WERE THE STEELERS' FIVE MOST MEMORABLE GAMES?

1 We're talking about a franchise that has won five Super Bowls, so the answer should be easy. That would be too easy, in fact. So let's eliminate the obvious from the discussion and focus on five games that didn't decide the NFL's championship.

5. 1975 AFC CHAMPIONSHIP VS. OAKLAND, JANUARY 4, 1976

The Steelers had plenty to overcome in this 16–10 victory. Not only did they have a tough opponent in the Raiders, they committed 8 turnovers and missed 2 field goals. Jack Lambert recovered 3 fumbles, including 2 in the fourth quarter. They led to 2 touchdowns, a 25-yard run by Franco Harris, and Terry Bradshaw's 20-yard pass to John Stallworth.

On top of it all, this was the famous frozen field game. The tarps at one side of the field at Three Rivers Stadium were not secured overnight and the artificial turf was icy at the start of the contest. Raiders owner Al Davis accused the Steelers of deliberately icing the field to take away Oakland's passing attack.

4. 2002 AFC WILD CARD GAME VS. CLEVELAND, JANUARY 5, 2003

The Steelers' defense didn't have much of a day, but the offense rallied for 4 touchdowns in the last 19 minutes and a 36–33 victory at Heinz Field. The Steelers recovered from a 17-point deficit, the biggest postseason comeback in franchise history. The Browns were unable to sit on their lead because they couldn't get a running game going to kill the clock. That gave the Steelers opportunities, and quarterback Tommy Maddox threw 3 touchdown passes to trim Cleveland's lead to 33–28. Maddox completed 30 of 48 passes for 367 yards and connected on 4 of his 5 attempts during the last drive. Chris Fuamatu-Ma'Afala ran 3 yards for the go-ahead touchdown with 54 seconds left in the fourth quarter. Antwaan Randle-El completed a pass to tight-end Jerame Tuman for the 2-point conversion. The Browns still nearly had a chance to tie the score. Andre King just missed getting out of bounds at the Pittsburgh 29-yard line before time expired.

3. 1995 AFC CHAMPIONSHIP VS. INDIANAPOLIS, JANUARY 14, 1996

This game came within inches of being one of the most devastating losses in Steelers history. The Steelers held a 10–6 halftime lead on Neil O'Donnell's 5-yard pass to Kordell Stewart and Norm Johnson's field goal. The Steelers had the ball at their own 33 yard line with 3:03 left after falling behind 16–13 on Jim Harbaugh's 47-yard touchdown pass to Floyd Turner. The Steelers converted on 4th down; then Ernie Mills was able to take a pass 37 yards to the 1-yard line. Bam Morris finished the drive with a touchdown that gave the Steelers a 20–16 lead. Indianapolis started the last drive at its own 16-yard line, but Harbaugh moved the team to the Pittsburgh 29-yard line with five seconds on the clock. He put a desperation pass up in the right corner of the end zone. Colts receiver Aaron Bailey nearly had the ball until defensive back Randy Fuller was able to knock it away, securing the game and sending the Steelers to the Super Bowl for the first time since 1979.

2. 2005 AFC PLAYOFFS AT INDIANAPOLIS, JANUARY 15, 2006

The Steelers shocked the favored Colts by jumping out to a quick 14–0 lead. The officials made the wrong call on what should have been an interception by Troy Polamalu (the NFL later acknowledged the mistake) and the Colts were able to get close at 21–18. The Steelers were at the Indianapolis 1-yard line, and appeared ready to seal the game. The celebration on the Pittsburgh sideline turned to panic when reliable Jerome Bettis fumbled as he neared the goal line. Cornerback Nick Harper recovered and looked as though he might return the ball for a Colts touchdown. But then quarterback Ben Roethlisberger was able to trip up Harper. The Colts still drove down the field, only to have kicker Mike Vanderjagt miss a 46-yard field goal with 18 seconds left in the fourth quarter. How stressful was the ending? One loyal Steelers fan, 50-year-old Terry O'Neill, suffered a heart attack while watching the game.

1. 1972 AFC PLAYOFFS, VS. OAKLAND, DECEMBER 23, 1972

This game represents a "Do you remember where you were when..." moment for a generation of Pittsburghers. It wasn't a great football game. The Steelers had an outstanding defense and not much offense. They were trailing 7–6 at their own 40-yard line with 22 seconds left in the fourth quarter. Bradshaw scrambled away from the rush, ducked under one tackler, and fired a pass downfield in the direction of Frenchy Fuqua. Defensive back Jack Tatum hit Fuqua and the ball caromed back, where Franco Harris grabbed it just before it hit the ground. Harris raced down the left sideline for a touchdown on the play that came to be known as "The Immaculate Reception." To this day some of the Raiders maintain the play was illegal (under the rules of the time, Harris couldn't catch the ball if it had hit Fuqua). Maybe that long-standing bitterness from Oakland makes the moment even sweeter for Steelers fans. It stands as the first great moment in the Steelers' 1970s success and remains one of the most unusual plays in NFL history.

DID THE STEELERS MAKE A MISTAKE BY NOT DRAFTING DAN MARINO?

2 This argument suggests the Steelers could have used a quarterback who would complete nearly 5,000 passes for more than 61,000 yards with 420 touchdowns over 17 seasons. While Marino was shredding the NFL record book on his way to the Hall of Fame from 1983 to 1999, the Steelers' quarterback parade included Cliff Stoudt, Mark Malone, David Woodley, Bubby Brister, Steve Bono, Todd Blackledge, Neil O'Donnell, Mike Tomczak, Jim Miller, and Kordell Stewart. Ouch.

The issue goes back to the fateful draft day in 1983 when the Steelers had the 21st overall pick and chose Texas Tech nose tackle Gabe Rivera. They felt a need to beef up a pass rush, and the 300-pound Rivera, nicknamed "Señor Sack," was a force. The 1983 draft saw six quarterbacks chosen in the first round, but the Steelers weren't in the market for one of them. They thought Terry Bradshaw still had some seasons left at age 35, and they also felt they'd drafted his eventual successor in 1980 when they selected Malone in the first round from Arizona State. Word was that Steelers founder Art Rooney favored drafting Marino, but the 82-year-old patriarch was far removed from the decision-making process by then.

Marino, Pittsburgh born and bred, was coming off a disappointing senior season at Pitt. He was also dogged by false rumors that he was involved with drugs. Even the first five teams searching for a quarterback passed on Marino. John Elway of Stanford was selected by Baltimore first overall. Then Penn State's Blackledge went to Kansas City seventh. Jim Kelly of Miami was the 14th selection by Buffalo, and New England selected Tony Eason of Illinois one turn later. In the 24th spot the New York Jets chose Ken O'Brien of Cal-Davis. Then, finally, the Miami Dolphins made Marino the 27th player chosen in the first round.

Perhaps getting away from Pittsburgh was the best thing that happened to Marino. Dolphins coach Don Shula liked to throw the ball, and Marino's strong arm and quick release were tailored for that style. He was installed as the starter (replacing Woodley) by the sixth game and led the Dolphins to the first of three division titles.

The Steelers' choice of Rivera turned into a tragedy six weeks into his rookie season, when he was paralyzed after a highway accident in Pittsburgh on October 20, 1983. The quarterback situation in Pittsburgh didn't offer a ray of light either: Bradshaw was sidelined by an elbow injury that would force him to retire just before the 1984 season.

He was followed by Stoudt, who had a passer rating of 60.6 in his one season as a starter before he fled for the now-defunct United States Football League (USFL). Malone was next in the series of inadequate replacements.

The Steelers eventually took a shot at getting Marino. In 1999, coach Bill Cowher called him about signing as a free agent. Miami coach Jimmy Johnson didn't seem to want Marino, and Cowher thought an experienced quarterback could get the Steelers into the Super Bowl. Marino carefully considered the offer, but decided to retire after spending his entire career with the Dolphins.

Maybe that was just as well. Had Steelers fans seen him wearing No. 13 in black and gold, they may have been tortured by the idea of what might have been had the Steelers' priorities been different in the 1983 draft.

WHO WERE THE STEELERS' MOST IMPORTANT FIRST-ROUND DRAFT PICKS?

3 The Steelers won four Super Bowls in six years, and the foundation of that dynasty came on six remarkable draft days. Nobody did a better job of getting talent out of the draft pool than the Steelers did in that stretch from 1969 to 1974.

There was no free agency in those days, and the Steelers were reluctant to make trades. That left the draft, and the Steelers had an excellent scouting department. Art Rooney Jr. led the scouting operations, assisted by Dick Haley and Bill Nunn, a former newspaperman whose network of contacts helped the Steelers find talent at small historically black colleges in the South that were often overlooked.

Here's a rundown of the five most important first-round choices in franchise history.

5. ROD WOODSON, CORNERBACK, PURDUE, DRAFTED TENTH OVERALL IN 1987

Woodson held out in a contract dispute for much of his rookie season, but he was worth the wait. A remarkable athlete who could have played on offense or defense, Woodson anchored the Steelers' secondary for a decade, and then prolonged his career with a move to safety for other teams after the Steelers miscalculated his value following a devastating knee injury. He was named to the NFL's All-Century team while he was still an active player, and is a lock for the Hall of Fame.

4. BEN ROETHLISBERGER, QUARTERBACK, MIAMI, OHIO, DRAFTED 11TH OVERALL IN 2004

The Steelers hadn't had a franchise-caliber quarterback since Terry Bradshaw retired after the 1983 season. Roethlisberger came in as a long-term project, but was pressed into service when starter Tommy Maddox was injured in the second game of the 2004 season. The Steelers simplified the offense for Roethlisberger, and he succeeded, going 13–0 as a starter before faltering in the postseason. In 2005, he became the youngest starting quarterback to win the Super Bowl at age 23.

3. TERRY BRADSHAW, QUARTERBACK, LOUISIANA TECH, DRAFTED FIRST OVERALL IN 1970

Only third place for a quarterback who won four Super Bowls? Yes, because it took a while for Bradshaw to get up to speed. He still wasn't established as the starter in his fifth season. He finally wrested the job from Joe Gilliam during the 1974 season. In the Steelers' first two Super Bowl seasons, Bradshaw handed off a lot more than he threw. He matured in later years and the NFL opened up the passing game, allowing the strong-armed Bradshaw to throw more and cement his Hall of Fame credentials.

2. JOE GREENE, DEFENSIVE TACKLE, NORTH TEXAS STATE, DRAFTED FOURTH OVERALL IN 1969

It's part of Steelers legend that a newspaper headline said "Joe Who?" on the day after Greene was selected. He answered that question almost immediately. Coach Chuck Noll called him "a fort on foot" and opponents soon discovered that a minimum of two blockers were needed to neutralize Greene. Notoriously hotheaded, he once flung the ball into the stands as a rookie, earning an ejection. That temper, however, also set a tone for a defense that would become one of the NFL's best in short order.

1. FRANCO HARRIS, RUNNING BACK, PENN STATE, DRAFTED 13TH OVERALL IN 1972

The Steelers knew they wanted a workhorse running back. The question was, which one? Noll favored the University of Houston's Robert Newhouse, apparently wary of scouting reports that suggested Harris didn't have the best work habits. The scouts prevailed, however, and the Steelers instantly got a credible running game. Harris, big yet shifty, was a sensation as a rookie, rushing for 1,055 yards and snagging the deflected pass in the playoffs that came to be known as the "Immaculate Reception," the most famous single play in Steelers history. Greene was vital to the defense, but Harris gets the top spot here because when he joined the team, the Steelers had enough offense to finally compete for a championship.

DID CHUCK NOLL STAY TOO LONG?

 The Steelers were created in the summer of 1933. They didn't get serious about winning until 36 years later.

The pivotal date in franchise history was January 27, 1969, when Chuck Noll was hired as head coach to replace Bill Austin. Noll was the first coach who had not been chosen by franchise founder Art Rooney. Rooney turned the responsibility over to his son Dan, which turned out to be an excellent idea. The Steelers had managed just eight winning seasons in the 36 years with Art Rooney in charge. They never won a championship and had appeared in only one postseason game, a playoff with Philadelphia to break a tie for the 1947 Eastern Division title. The Steelers lost, 21–0.

Noll had an impressive résumé. He had played under Paul Brown at Cleveland, broke into coaching as an assistant to Sid Gillman in San Diego, and was fresh from serving as Don Shula's top aide with the Baltimore Colts. Noll was smart, driven, and confident. In his first meeting with the team, he told them things would change, and that it was unlikely many of them would be staying with the Steelers.

It took three seasons to weed out players and draft better replacements, but in 1972, the Steelers won their first division title and started a stretch of eight consecutive playoff seasons. Two years after that they won the first of four Super Bowls in six seasons. Noll had not only erased the painful acronym SOS (Same Old Steelers), he had built a dynasty.

The run ended with a 9–7 season in 1980 that saw the Steelers miss the playoffs. It was the start of a trend. Over his last 12 years, Noll's record was 93–91, with just four playoff seasons. On November 14, 1988, *Sports Illustrated* ran a cover that pictured Noll and Dallas's Tom Landry with

13

a headline asking if they had lost their touch; the Steelers were 2–7 the week the issue was published. Whatever patience ownership still had with Noll seemed to diminish after a 5–11 1988 season, when Dan Rooney ordered Noll to fire three assistant coaches. A fourth, Tony Dungy, resigned rather than accept a demotion from his position as defensive coordinator.

It wasn't the technical aspects that had gotten away from Noll. No, his biggest problem came in judging talent. The Steelers had a series of terrible first-round draft picks who contributed little. The list included defensive linemen Aaron Jones (1988) and Darryl Sims (1985), offensive tackle John Rienstra (1986), running back Tim Worley (1989), and linebacker Huey Richardson (1991).

Noll also misjudged talent on the sidelines. He hired former New York Jets head coach Joe Walton as his offensive coordinator in 1990 and soon had a player mutiny. Instead of having Walton change his terminology to conform with the Steelers' existing language, Noll allowed Walton to keep his system and forced the players to learn the new lingo. Quarterback Bubby Brister was among those complaining the loudest, setting a tone for the offense to reject Walton's ideas.

The issue died with Noll's retirement four days after the 1991 season ended. Rather than force a struggle with personnel director Tom Donahoe (it was an open secret that Donahoe was critical of Noll and was lobbying for more authority), Noll retired after 23 seasons and a few weeks short of his 60th birthday. Less than a month after Noll left, the Steelers hired Bill Cowher as head coach. The Steelers benefited from the change, making the playoffs in each of Cowher's first six seasons.

So did Noll stay too long? Probably, given his reluctance to reduce his authority in personnel matters. Under his reign, the Steelers dynasty dwindled into a series of average teams.

WHY IS STEELERS FOUNDER ART ROONEY SO BELOVED?

5 Arthur J. Rooney had great timing. His greatest accomplishments with the Steelers came late in his life, which gave everyone warm and fuzzy feelings about the white-haired grandfather with thick glasses who was nicknamed "The Chief."

Pittsburgh wasn't always that crazy about Rooney, though, especially when the Steelers failed to win through the franchise's first 39 seasons. The cry was often that Rooney was too cheap to field a championship-caliber team, but that was a bad rap. Rooney spent money. He just didn't run the organization very well. He relied on his NFL cronies for recommendations, which is how he wound up with Bill Austin, who coached the team to an 11–28–3 record from 1966 to 1968. Austin had been enthusiastically endorsed by Vince Lombardi, and that was good enough for Rooney. It turned out, however, that Austin's efforts to duplicate Lombardi's dictatorial style were a disaster.

The consistent failure was surprising because, unlike a lot of owners, Rooney knew sports. He had been an athlete and came from the rough streets of Pittsburgh's North Side. In addition to playing semi-pro football, he trained as a boxer, won two Amatuer Athletic Union (AAU) titles, and was selected for the 1920 U.S. Olympic boxing team. He played minor league baseball until an arm injury ended his career. He loved the race track, and folklore—now debunked—held that he founded the Steelers with the $2,500 he won during a hot streak of betting on horses.

Rooney finally helped turn the team into a winning organization when he took a step back and let his sons run the franchise. Dan Rooney hired Chuck Noll as head coach and Art Rooney Jr. headed the scouting department that drafted most of the players who won four Super Bowls in six years.

Despite the wealth the soaring Steelers brought as the value of NFL franchises exploded, Rooney was without pretense. The only people he disliked were the ones who tried to act like big shots. He stayed on the North Side long after the neighborhood had declined. He was embarrassed when he overheard a receptionist answer the phone "World Champion Steelers," and immediately told her that the standard "Steelers" would suffice. He declined sweetheart offers to move the Steelers to Sunbelt cities that lusted for an NFL franchise. His sense of decency was profound. When his wife died, he took many of the floral arrangements to other rooms in the funeral home and gave them to other grieving families.

Rooney enjoyed visiting with the sportswriters daily in the small press room at Three Rivers Stadium. In 1986, the Steelers were desperate for a running back and signed free agent Earnest Jackson. Soon after that transaction, Rooney made his usual stop in the press room, but found everyone too busy to talk because they were chasing details about Jackson. Rooney watched the frenzy for a few seconds, smiled, and softly said, "You know, this isn't Gale Sayers that we signed."

Rooney's down-to-earth personality brought him friends from all walks of life. At Rooney's order, the Steelers took two members of the stadium grounds crew on every road trip. When he went on trips to his beloved Ireland, hundreds of his friends received postcards that he wrote, addressed, stamped, and mailed himself. He loved to have Joe Greene and Terry Bradshaw stop by his office for a cigar and conversation after practice.

Rooney died on August 25, 1988, at 87, and people lined

up for blocks to pay their respects. There was live television coverage of his funeral. Sportswriter Gene Collier coauthored a play about Rooney's life, and "The Chief" has played to full houses for several runs over the past three years. There's even talk of a DVD version of the production. Only in Pittsburgh? Maybe, but even then only for someone as rich in character as Arthur J. Rooney.

WHAT IF THE STEELERS HAD TO CHOOSE?

The Steelers' Super Bowl dynasty of the 1970s was built on six incredibly productive years in the draft, 1969–1974. The Steelers assembled a strong core group of players in those drafts and won the Super Bowl four times in the six years from 1974 to 1979.

And they were able to hold on to the talented players because the NFL didn't have free agency. Aside from the distraction created by the short-lived World Football League in 1974–1975, players had nowhere else to go.

Today there's free agency and a salary cap system that forces teams to make tough choices. Had the system been in effect in the 1970s, the Steelers probably wouldn't have been able to keep two Hall-of-Fame-caliber players at the same position. The cap system requires teams to spread the wealth, and that usually means one superstar salary at each position.

If the Steelers had to choose, which eventual Hall of Famer would they keep? Let's start at linebacker.

6 JACK HAM OR JACK LAMBERT?

Ham arrived first as a second-round pick from Penn State in 1971. Andy Russell, who played linebacker alongside Lambert and Ham, recalled a drill from Ham's rookie season. The outside linebackers were expected to read keys on every play and react according to what they saw. Russell said that Ham had a perfect score in the drill, which often confused veterans.

There was a matter-of-fact style to everything that Ham did, and perhaps that sometimes blunted the appreciation his skills deserved. He was always in the right place at the right time, making plays that rarely seemed to be spectacular. But his preparation and understanding of the game allowed him to be effective with a certain air of nonchalance. Ham wasn't physically imposing at 225 pounds, but he was quick and powerful. Ham would drop a running back for a loss, turn, and return to his huddle. There was no celebratory dance, no chest thumping. He was doing his job.

Lambert, on the other hand, was far more conspicuous, although not by design. Lambert had the habit of pumping his legs in anticipation of the play, and TV cameras picked up on the tic and exploited it. He was colorful in the literal sense as well—Lambert's hands would bleed when he grabbed players to make tackles, and he would habitually wipe his hands on his pants. His bright gold pants were always spotted red. To an outsider, Lambert looked like a predator who was stained by the blood of his victims. He was fast enough that the Steelers could use him in pass coverage, and, given his tall and lean figure with stringy blonde hair and piercing eyes, Lambert intimidated. And for good reason. When Roy Gerela missed a field goal in Super Bowl X, Cliff Harris of the Dallas Cowboys sarcastically patted him on the helmet. Lambert saw that action, charged Harris, and threw him to the turf.

Drafted in the second round in 1974, Lambert came from Kent State with plenty to prove. He hadn't played in a big-time college program, but he wasn't daunted by the NFL. As soon as the Steelers drafted him, he showed up at the team's offices to watch films and get familiar with the systems. Lambert's break came when incumbent middle linebacker Henry Davis suffered a concussion in the preseason that ultimately forced him to retire. Lambert took over the important spot and the team went to its first Super Bowl in his rookie season.

He took control of the mental game as well—Lambert

once delivered a two-handed shove to the chest of teammate Joe Greene when he heard something he didn't like on the sideline. Lambert would stand up to anyone and challenge teammates if he thought they were short-changing on effort.

In some ways, Ham's clinical approach caused his physical toughness to be shortchanged. Similarly, those who saw Lambert only as a hulking presence missed all the film study and preparation that allowed him to be in position to make plays.

Both Ham and Lambert were superb players. If the Steelers could only keep one, though, the choice would be Lambert, by the absolute slimmest of margins. The tiebreaker would be the emotional leadership he provided to the team. But if it came down to a choice, it would be worth pleading the case to the team accountants to find a way to keep both.

7 LYNN SWANN OR JOHN STALLWORTH?

These two talented receivers came from the 1974 draft. Swann was the first-round choice, and Stallworth was chosen in the fourth round. Coach Chuck Noll was so impressed with Stallworth that he was willing to take him in the first round. But the scouts assured Noll that Stallworth would last until later, so the Steelers wound up with a pair of Hall of Fame receivers from the same draft.

Swann had taken dance lessons as a child, and that

grace and balance showed in his play. He made spectacular leaping catches and perfected a sliding catch that made the low pass almost impossible to intercept. He never had more than 880 receiving yards in a season, but that comes with a couple of disclaimers. For a lot of his career (1974–1982), the Steelers were a run-first team built around Franco Harris. When things opened up and the Steelers threw the ball more, Swann and Stallworth were number 1 and number 1-A, respectively, and the passes were divided between them.

Swann wasn't big, but he was tough. He was dealt a concussion in the 1975 AFC championship game. That didn't stop him from playing in the Super Bowl two weeks later, though, and it didn't make him shy about going over the middle to make catches. Critics who wouldn't support his Hall of Fame candidacy argued that Swann didn't have enough receptions, but he had some of his biggest games in the Steelers' four Super Bowls and was the Most Valuable Player of Super Bowl X.

Stallworth had three 1,000-yard receiving seasons and wound up as the Steelers' career leader with 8,723 receiving yards from 1974 to 1987. He had excellent speed and leaping ability. Stallworth was steady without being spectacular. He was a reliable receiver with great hands who could get into the open and make yards after the catch. He and Swann complemented each other. Because Stallworth's career lasted five years longer than Swann's, he was around for the parade of lesser quarterbacks who followed Terry Bradshaw. The Steelers' passing game was in less-than-high gear with Cliff Stoudt and Mark Malone at the controls, and Stallworth saw fewer opportunities as the years went by.

It all comes down to the Super Bowls. In four games, Stallworth caught 11 passes for 268 yards, including 73 yards on one pivotal catch against the Los Angeles Rams in Super Bowl XIV. Swann, on the other hand, had 364 receiving yards and 398 all-purpose yards.   Forced to choose one, the pick would be Swann, although Stallworth is still an excellent 1-A and a first-rate runner-up.

8 LYNN SWANN OR HINES WARD?

Let's branch a little further out in this vein, to include some of today's players in our debate. Swann and Ward are the top receivers of two distinctly different generations of Steelers. But which one is better? Let's see how they match up.

Swann was the favorite target of Terry Bradshaw in the 1970s, and the two worked together almost exclusively. Swann came in as the first-round draft choice in 1974, the same year that Bradshaw took the starting job from Joe Gilliam and finally made it his own. Except for injury absences, Bradshaw remained the starter through 1982, which was also Swann's last season.

Ward joined the Steelers as a third-round selection in

1998. He's had Kordell Stewart, Mike Tomczak, Kent Graham, Tommy Maddox, and Ben Roethlisberger as his starting quarterbacks through his first nine seasons.

Swann is best remembered for his leaping acrobatic catches, but he was also a tough competitor who wasn't afraid to make catches in the middle of the field. Ward's toughness is legendary. He bounces up from jarring tackles with a smile on his face, and defensive backs have complained about the devastating blocks he throws on some Steelers' running plays. His competitiveness wears on opponents.

Swann was a sure-handed receiver, as is Ward. Swann had more speed and overall quickness, but Ward isn't especially lacking in either category. Swann played in a time when defensive players could take more physical liberties with receivers, but Ward is one of the current players who wouldn't have had a problem playing under the old rules.

Swann was a valuable punt returner in his rookie season. By his second season, he had been excused from that dangerous duty and became full-time receiver. Ward has limited experience in returning kickoffs for the Steelers.

The tiebreaker here is Ward's versatility. He gives the Steelers offensive coordinators a chance to include some game-changing gadget plays because of his ability to run *and* pass the ball. (Ward played quarterback in high school and has thrown a couple of option passes in his NFL career.) But probably the biggest benefit is his ability and willingness to block. Ward attacks the job with enthusiasm, and that often is an unseen factor in the success of the Steelers' running game.

Swann is deservedly a Hall of Famer, but Ward will be there one day, too. Because of his versatility, Ward is the pick.

9 FRANCO HARRIS OR JEROME BETTIS?

This brings us to another past/present discussion. Franco Harris and Jerome Bettis are number 1 and number 2, respectively, in career rushing yards with the Steelers, two workhorse backs who each led a run-oriented offense in two different eras.

Harris came to the Steelers in one of the best draft-day decisions the organization ever made. Bettis was acquired in one of the best trades in franchise history.

Harris was taller, at 6 feet 2 inches, and 240 pounds. Bettis was a bowling ball stuffed into black and gold, just 5 feet 11 inches and probably about 260 pounds at his peak (Bettis's actual playing weight was always a well-guarded Steelers secret).

Critics complained that Harris would run out of bounds when he had the chance, avoiding collisions that might have gotten him an extra yard. No one ever made that claim about Bettis, who would slam into the center of the line with little regard for the toll that contact would take on his body.

Harris was the Steelers' first-round pick in 1972, after a college career at Penn State that raised some doubts. Some scouts saw him as lazy; Harris rarely displayed emotion on the field. He ran hard, but otherwise had a languid nature that sometimes showed in his body language. Scouts and coaches who are naturally drawn to overt fieriness wouldn't come away with a good first impression of Harris. Steelers scouts looked deeper and saw a talented runner who, despite his size, had the ability to shift and make tacklers miss. Harris had good speed and his hands were sure enough to make him a pass-catching threat out of the backfield.

He was installed in the Steelers lineup and immediately upgraded the offense. Harris became the fourth rookie in NFL history to rush for 1,000 yards. He took his success in stride and quietly built on it. The Steelers won their first Super Bowl in his third season, and Harris was the Most Valuable Player of the game after running for a then-record 158 yards with a touchdown. Harris was a mainstay throughout the Steelers' Super Bowl years and outlasted many of his contemporaries (maybe there was some value in stepping out of bounds now and then?).

Bettis was available in 1996 because the St. Louis Rams had soured on his attitude. If that's not a bizarre enough misjudgment, consider that the Rams promptly replaced him with Lawrence Phillips, the former Nebraska running back who was best known for his rap sheet of violent crimes. Bettis solved an immediate need as running back for the Steelers and energized the team with his slamming style. After an especially good run, he'd bounce up and do a little sideways dance back to the huddle. Bettis turned his nickname "The Bus" into a persona that he used for merchandising opportunities. His gregarious nature made him perfect for a weekly TV show in which he had team-mates as guests.

Harris' career ended because of an ill-advised contract holdout. The Steelers released him and he spent a season with Seattle. Bettis was also involved in contract issues at the end of his career. The wear and tear was catching up with him, and the Steelers thought Bettis was no longer worth either the salary his contract commanded or a start-ing spot. He renegotiated and gave back millions to stay on the team. When his replacement, Duce Staley, was injured, Bettis again took the starting role.

Harris wound up with 11,950 rushing yards from 1972 to 1983. Bettis ran for 10,571 yards from 1996 to2005. Harris ran for 91 touchdowns; Bettis had 78. Bettis had fifty 100-yard games to Harris's 47.

Harris is in the Hall of Fame, and Bettis will join him as soon as he becomes eligible.

The tiebreaker between these two is Harris's longevity. He was the Steelers' leading rusher for 12 consecutive seasons, twice as long as Bettis had that role. In 1974, the first Super Bowl season, Harris carried the ball 208 times for 1,006 yards. The Steelers threw the ball only 277 times for 1,177 yards. The offense was more balanced in Bettis's years. There was only one season (1997) in which the Steelers' team passing yardage wasn't more than double the number of yards Bettis gained on the ground.

Harris is the choice, but it's hard to imagine a better backup option than Bettis.

WERE STEROIDS THE STEELERS' SECRET WEAPON IN THE 1970s?

Pittsburgh fans like to lambaste Barry Bonds as a steroids cheater, but they take strong umbrage when anyone suggests the Steelers of the 1970s used performance-enhancing drugs.

The issue came to a head when western Pennsylvania native and former Steelers assistant coach Jim Haslett said in 2005 that it was common knowledge the Steelers of the 1970s were at the forefront of steroid use. Haslett admitted he took steroids in the early 1980s when he was a linebacker with the Buffalo Bills.

"It started, really, in Pittsburgh," Haslett told the media during the 2005 NFL owners' meetings. "They got an advantage on a lot of football teams. They were so much stronger (in the) '70s, late '70s, early '80s. They're the ones who kind of started it."

Of course, the timeframe Haslett outlined coincides with the Steelers' stretch of four Super Bowl championships in six years from 1974 to1979. Any disparaging comments about those teams are automatically fighting words in Pittsburgh. Steelers chairman Dan Rooney denied Haslett's allegations, even telling the *Pittsburgh Post-Gazette* that "maybe (steroids) affected his mind." Former coach Chuck Noll, via Rooney, has turned down all requests for comment on the issue. Jon Kolb, an offensive lineman on the Super Bowl teams, said he wasn't even aware of steroids until he participated in a made-for-TV World's Strongest Man competition in 1980. Kolb said he met athletes who had used steroids during that event. Lou Riecke, the Steelers' strength coach from 1970 to 1980, told the *Pittsburgh Post-Gazette*, "I'll guarantee you I was not aware that anybody was taking them. It was never even discussed. I didn't see it."

But the presence of at least some steroids has been noted by several accounts. Rocky Bleier, the running back who bulked up noticeably during his career, has said he took steroids, but with a doctor's prescription as part of his recovery from Vietnam War wounds. When the family of the late Mike Webster sued the NFL Pension Fund, two doctors gave statements saying that Webster, the Steelers' center from 1974 to1988, had "experimented" with steroids. And then there is a matter-of-fact admission of steroid use from former offensive guard Jim Clack in Roy Blount's 1974 book, *About Three Bricks Shy of a Load*. Clack recounted how steroids helped him quickly gain weight and strength in the months between the 1971 draft and the start of training camp. He said he stopped using them because his wife was concerned about possible long-term health problems.

Former offensive guard Steve Courson was most outspoken about steroids. He was considered an authority on the subject, from his personal history and the study he'd devoted to the topic after he developed serious heart problems that he traced to his steroid usage. (Courson died at age fifty on November 10, 2005, when a tree he was cutting down shifted direction and fell on him.)

Courson revealed that he started using steroids as a college player at South Carolina. When he arrived at the Steelers camp as a rookie in 1977, he had the tell-tale "inflated" physique. Courson did a confessional interview with *Sports Illustrated* in 1985 about his own steroid use, a precursor to his book on the subject, *False Glory*, published in 1991. He suggested in the book that 75 percent of the Steelers' offensive linemen had used steroids. Courson said steroids were enough of an open secret that players would often discuss their dosages and cycles in casual locker room conversations.

He wrote, "Disgruntled players throughout the league called us the 'Steroid Team,' as if performance-enhancing drugs were the sole reason for our success. The fact is our steroid usage was the same—give or take—as the rest of the NFL teams at that time." Courson said Noll never openly condoned steroids but, "conveniently and most definitely turned his head."

The NFL started testing for steroids in 1987, but the system has loopholes that can be easily exploited. It would be incredibly naïve to think that steroids weren't prevalent before testing went into effect. Although few players of that era have gone on the record, some have, and there is a mountain of circumstantial evidence, such as players suddenly shrinking to normal proportions after their playing careers ended.

There can be little doubt that some Steelers used steroids in the 1970s. But as Courson, the most credible source on the subject, said, they were hardly alone. Did it really represent an edge if everyone was doing it?

WHAT WAS THE BIGGEST MISTAKE THE STEELERS EVER MADE?

The 1960s were a bleak period for the Steelers, who had two winning seasons and a 46–85–7 record. Why? Because they spent most of the decade looking for a good quarterback.

Most weekends they could look to Baltimore and regret their decision to cut Johnny Unitas after barely giving him a chance in their 1955 training camp. Unitas, a native of Pittsburgh's Mt. Washington section, was a ninth-round draft choice from Louisville. He was the number-4 quarterback in camp, stuck behind Jim Finks, Ted Marchibroda, and Vic Eaton. Finks and Marchibroda were fine NFL players. Eaton owed his third-string status to the fact he could also punt.

Coach Walt Kiesling was unimpressed with what little he saw of Unitas. He complained that Unitas was awkward and couldn't remember the plays. Unitas never got on the field in the exhibition season, and therefore it was no surprise when he was cut three weeks before the season opened. Who was going to notice a seldom-used, low-round draft pick?

Unitas went home and took a construction job. He kept his football skills sharp by playing in Pittsburgh for the semi-pro Bloomfield Rams, who paid him $6 a game. Someone tipped off the Baltimore Colts about a quarterback who was playing on the sandlots in Pittsburgh. The Colts extended Unitas an opportunity to try out in 1956, and the rest is NFL history. Unitas became one of the game's best at a time when quarterbacks were required to call their own plays. He may not have looked like an athlete, but he was cool under pressure, threw precise passes, and had exceptional leadership skills. The Colts were a consistent contender with Unitas at quarterback.

The Steelers weren't so lucky. Their 1955 surplus wasn't as deep as they thought, and they went through a parade of quarterbacks. Finks retired after the 1955 season and was replaced by Marchibroda. Marchibroda spent just one season as the Steelers' starter. He completed only 45 percent of his passes and threw more interceptions (19) than touchdowns (12). Eaton lasted just one season, 1955, with the Steelers.

It didn't get much better—the Steelers made plenty of other mistakes. Len Dawson from Purdue was the Steelers' number-one draft pick in 1957, and quarterbacks Jack Kemp and Earl Morrall would also pass through Pittsburgh in that same season. Both were acquired in trades. Dawson spent three seasons with the Steelers but played sparingly. He backed up Morrall as a rookie. When Morrall was traded to Detroit to acquire Bobby Layne, Dawson watched Layne start. The Steelers finally traded Dawson to Cleveland on December 31, 1959, to get a receiver, Preston Carpenter. The Steelers didn't see Dawson unseating Layne, and they needed help at receiver. Nothing changed for Dawson in Cleveland, where he continued to stand on the sideline. In Dawson's first five NFL seasons, he started two games. He never started and finished a game. His career didn't blossom until he went to the American Football League with the Dallas Texans in 1962. The franchise became the Kansas City Chiefs the following season, and Dawson was their star. He led the Chiefs to three AFL titles and an upset of the Minnesota Vikings in Super Bowl IV. Dawson was elected to the Pro Football Hall of Fame in 1987.

Morrall was never a superstar, but he was a steady pro who played through 1977. The Steelers dealt him to get Layne, who wound up retiring after the 1962 season. Morrall was the NFL's Most Valuable Player in 1968 when he filled in for the injured Unitas and took Baltimore to the Super Bowl. He also played for the undefeated 1972 Miami Dolphins when starter Bob Griese was injured, and was voted the league's comeback player of the year.

Like Dawson, Kemp found a home in the AFL and quarterbacked the Buffalo Bills to a pair of league titles. Kemp appeared in only 4 games for the Steelers in 1957, attempting 18 passes. He was cut after the season.

Back to Unitas. Steelers founder Art Rooney's sons were serving as ballboys in training camp and were amazed at Unitas's passing accuracy in workouts. Tim Rooney felt so strongly about keeping Unitas that he wrote an 11-page letter to his father, imploring him to overrule the coaches and find a place for Unitas on the roster. Dad's reply: "Why don't you leave the coaching to the coaches?"

Shortly after Unitas was cut, Rooney and son Dan were caught in traffic. Dan Rooney waved to someone in a passing car. Art Rooney asked who it was, and Dan said it was Unitas. Art Rooney told his son to catch up to the car at the next light. Art Rooney rolled down his window, got Unitas's attention and said, "Good luck, John. I hope you get a chance somewhere else."

Unitas got that chance, and the Steelers spent many years regretting the biggest mistake they ever made.

DID THE STEELERS HIRE MIKE TOMLIN BECAUSE OF THE "ROONEY RULE"?

12 Bill Cowher's 2006 resignation sent the Steelers on a rare search for a new head coach. It was just the second time since 1969 that they'd been in the market for a coach: Cowher had replaced Chuck Noll, who had held the job from 1969 through the 1991 season.

The Steelers had two strong candidates in-house: offensive coordinator Ken Whisenhunt had turned down the Oakland Raiders a year earlier and offensive line coach/assistant head coach Russ Grimm had also interviewed for several head coaching jobs. To round out the interviewing process the Steelers brought in Mike Tomlin, the Minnesota Vikings' defensive coordinator, and Ron Rivera, who held the same position with the Chicago Bears. Chan Gailey of Georgia Tech, a former Steelers assistant who had coached the Dallas Cowboys, was a late entry. Gailey was apparently recommended by Cowher.

Every team is obligated to interview minority candidates

for head coaching jobs. That NFL diversity policy was pushed by Steelers chairman Dan Rooney at league meetings, and came to be known throughout the league as the "Rooney Rule." The Steelers were in compliance with the edict because Tomlin is African American and Rivera is Hispanic.

The Arizona Cardinals offered Whisenhunt their head coaching job and he accepted without waiting to see what happened with the Steelers. The Steelers then announced they had three finalists: Grimm, Tomlin, and Rivera. They were forbidden from giving Rivera a second interview because he was occupied with the Bears' run to the Super Bowl. That realistically left Grimm and Tomlin, and that's when things got interesting.

On Saturday, January 20, several national news reports said Tomlin had been selected. Meanwhile, the Pittsburgh *Tribune-Review* ran a front-page story in its Sunday, January 21 edition, citing unnamed sources who said Grimm had been offered the job and accepted it. The Steelers denied a choice had been made. On January 21, the Steelers contacted Tomlin and formally offered him a four-year contract with a team option for a fifth season.

Because of all the last-minute confusions, some media outlets suggested that the Steelers had been pressured by the NFL and the NFL Players Association to hire a minority candidate as a way of backing the "Rooney Rule" with action. The Rooneys, however, denied that race played a big role in their choice.

No doubt there were hints that hiring Tomlin would be a plus for the league and its diversity program. But Dan Rooney's history indicates he lets nothing get in the way of business. He once fired his brother, Art Rooney Jr., who ran the Steelers' scouting department in the 1970s. Despite the public perception of Whisenhunt and Grimm as the favorites, apparently the Steelers never felt that way. If the Steelers had wanted Grimm that badly, they would have hired him, regardless of outside influences. The Steelers have always stubbornly stuck to doing things their way and resisting outside pressures. Tomlin was hired because the interview process convinced them he was the best candidate.

WHO WERE THE STEELERS' FIVE GREATEST "SLEEPER" DRAFT PICKS?

The NFL draft has become a major event, complete with all-day television coverage and countless hours devoted to previewing and analyzing the process. In the past, the draft was a low-key affair conducted in relative obscurity—not because teams were hiding secrets, but because there weren't that many people who paid attention. It was even low on the players' radar. When a friend told University of Missouri linebacker Andy Russell he'd just been drafted in 1963, his immediate reaction was to wonder why his student status didn't exempt him from being called to military duty.

The draft started in 1936, and at times there have been as many as 30 rounds. Since 1992, the draft has been limited to seven rounds, currently conducted over two days. For the purposes of a "sleeper," we're going to go back a bit, looking at anyone taken in the tenth round or later. There were 17 rounds from 1967 to 1976, then 12 rounds through 1992.

Some good candidates don't make our top five: Brady Keys (14th round, 1960) was a solid defensive back for a decade and tackle John Jackson (tenth round, 1988) was a key part of the Steelers' offensive line for ten years. Merril Hoge (tenth round in 1987) ran for 3,115 yards over seven seasons. But there are better sleepers. Following are the top five.

5. FRANK POLLARD, 11th ROUND, 1980, BAYLOR

Pollard was the Steelers' leading rusher in the first two seasons after Franco Harris left Pittsburgh. His 3,989 yards are fourth on the Steelers' career list, trailing Harris, Jerome Bettis, and John Henry Johnson. His average of 4.2 yards per carry is slightly better than the averages of Harris (4.1) and Bettis (3.9).

4. ROCKY BLEIER, 16th ROUND, 1968, NOTRE DAME

The Steelers took a chance on this undersized running back, who rewarded their patience with a 1,036-yard season in 1976. Bleier was also a reliable pass catcher out of the backfield. Bleier, who overcame war wounds sustained while serving in Vietnam, was also an exceptional blocker who helped open lanes for Franco Harris.

3. MIKE WAGNER, 11th ROUND, 1971, WESTERN ILLINOIS

Wagner was an often overlooked member of the defense that won four Super Bowls. He was a fierce hitter at the safety position from 1971 to 1980 and earned a spot in two Pro Bowls. Wagner had 36 career interceptions.

2. ANDY RUSSELL, 16th ROUND, 1963, MISSOURI

Russell had no aspirations to play professional football because his father thought it was a waste of time. Russell joined the Steelers after convincing his family he would use his NFL earnings to finance an advanced degree. He

got the degree, but he also played through 1976, partici-
pating in seven Pro Bowls. He was the only NFL linebacker
to make the Pro Bowl all six years from 1971 to 1976.
Russell retired prematurely to manage his burgeoning
investment business. The Steelers tried unsuccessfully to
coax him back.

1. L. C. GREENWOOD, 10th ROUND, 1969, ARKANSAS AM & N

The Steelers got half of their front four at opposite ends of
the 1969 draft. They took Joe Greene in the first round and
grabbed Greenwood much later. Why was he still
available? Some teams were wary of a knee injury in his
senior year. Plus, Greenwood weighed only 225 pounds.
This was considered too light to play the defensive line in
the NFL, and a couple of teams considered switching him
to an outside linebacker spot. But the Steelers liked the
rangy 6-foot, 6-inch Greenwood as an unconventional pass
rusher from the end position, and their projection was
correct. He made six Pro Bowls, led the Steelers in sacks
six times, and had 73.5 sacks in his 13 seasons. Greenwood
has been a finalist twice in voting for the Pro Football Hall
of Fame.

WHAT WERE THE STEELERS' FIVE WORST FIRST-ROUND DRAFT PICKS?

The Steelers showed in the 1970s that good drafting can set a team up for years of success. Of course, draft mistakes will cause problems for years, too.

This collection of failed first-rounders is deliberately geared more toward recent times. Drafting in the early days of the NFL included some scouting and a lot of guess-work. There were times when teams would take players from local colleges to have an attraction who could help sell tickets. The process has become more of a science these days. Teams build a video library of top candidates, they watch workouts, they conduct personal interviews, and they rely on psychological testing. Despite all the preparation, there are still first-round busts. Here are the Steelers' most regrettable first-round choices.

5. DICK LEFTRIDGE, RUNNING BACK, WEST VIRGINIA, FOURTH OVERALL IN 1966

Leftridge was one of the first African Americans to attend West Virginia on a full athletic scholarship, and he was a standout for the Mountaineers. The Steelers were looking for a running back to replace the retired John Henry Johnson, and they selected Leftridge. He lasted one season, in which he carried the ball just eight times for 17 yards and 2 touchdowns. They got much more use out of another rookie, Bill Asbury, who led the team with 544 yards and 7 touchdowns. Unfortunately, they could have drafted Mike Garrett, who signed with Kansas City. They did draft Emerson Boozer in the seventh round in 1966, but he opted to sign with the New York Jets in the last year of separate NFL and AFL drafting.

4. DARRYL SIMS, DEFENSIVE TACKLE, WISCONSIN, 20th OVERALL IN 1985

It seemed like the Steelers spent most of the decade looking for the kind of dominant defensive lineman that Joe Greene was in the Super Bowl era. Sims was among the many who tried and failed in that role. He didn't seem to have the aggressiveness or quickness to succeed. He was gone after two undistinguished seasons. He's best remembered for his response to a newspaper profile that asked for his favorite color. He chose plaid.

3. JAMAIN STEPHENS, OFFENSIVE TACKLE, NORTH CAROLINA AT & T, 29th OVERALL IN 1996

The worst pick of the Bill Cowher era was Jamain Stephens, a lineman from a small school who never adjusted to the NFL. The Steelers knew he might be a project when they selected him, but they didn't realize how ill equipped he was for the challenge. Stephens was cut when he failed to complete a running drill in his last training camp. Ironically, the day he was drafted was one of the most memorable in the Cowher era, too. The Steelers traded their number-2 draft pick to St. Louis and got running back Jerome Bettis.

2. BOB FERGUSON, RUNNING BACK, OHIO STATE, THIRD OVERALL IN 1962

Ferguson appeared to be an incredibly safe pick. He was a bruising running back who had put up big numbers in a major college program. He gained 2,162 yards at Ohio State and was the school's number-2 career rusher when he finished his career with the Buckeyes. But none of that translated to the NFL. Injuries slowed Ferguson, who lasted two seasons with the Steelers, then finished with the Minnesota Vikings. He played only 25 NFL games over three seasons. In his 18 games with the Steelers, he carried the ball 63 times for 208 yards and 1 touchdown.

1. HUEY RICHARDSON, LINEBACKER, FLORIDA, 15th OVERALL IN 1991

The mistake of all mistakes, Richardson was too small to play on the defensive line and not quick enough to play outside linebacker. The Steelers were impressed with the school record of 12.5 sacks he had posted as a junior and envisioned him as a strong pass rusher. That never happened, and he was cut after two seasons. Richardson also failed in brief trials with the New York Jets and Washington Redskins.

The worst part is that Brett Favre and Rickey Watters were both on the draft board when the Steelers selected Richardson. If they wanted a linebacker, they could have had Mo Lewis, who lasted until the 63rd overall pick. The bottom line on Richardson came from former Steelers defensive coordinator Dave Brazil, who told the *Pittsburgh Post-Gazette*: "He just wasn't a football player."

Given the importance of the first round, you like to get a football player.

WHO WAS THE MOST DANGEROUS COACH IN STEELERS HISTORY?

On the surface, Raymond K. "Buddy" Parker's eight-year run as Steelers head coach appears to have been successful.

He is one of four coaches (Bill Cowher, Chuck Noll, and Jock Sutherland are the others) to post a winning record with the Steelers. Parker was 51–48–6 for a .514 winning percentage from 1957 to 1964. But that modest success was undermined by Parker's impulsiveness, which was a big reason the coaches after him had such a tough time in the 1960s.

Parker arrived in 1957 after coaching the Detroit Lions to a pair of NFL championships during a six-year stay there. He abruptly quit the Lions during training camp in 1957. Two weeks later the Steelers hired him, pushing Walt Kiesling aside.

The hastiness that led him to announce his resignation at a fan banquet in Detroit would become part of Parker's profile in Pittsburgh, too. After a tough loss on the road, he'd pace the aisle of the airplane telling players they were cut. After a loss in Detroit, Parker placed his entire team on waivers.

Eventually the players realized the emotional Parker was just blowing off steam, and they came to ignore him.

But there were some player personnel moves that he didn't rescind. Parker was famous for trading prime draft picks for immediate stopgap help. He only saw draft picks as an abstract concept that might help down the road. They might even wind up helping a different Steelers coach. His philosophy was that he needed help right now, so why not deal a pick to plug a hole in the lineup? Other teams were delighted to do business with the Steelers. They knew they could unload a veteran near the end of the line and get a high-round draft choice in return. When the Steelers lost, other coaches knew Parker would be in the mood to make changes, and they'd call to propose trades.

In 1963, the Steelers didn't draft a player until the eighth round, when they took Stanford tackle Frank Atkinson. Parker had traded the first seven picks to Chicago, Baltimore, Green Bay, Chicago, Los Angeles, Chicago, and Green Bay. Among the players available in that draft were future Hall of Famers Bobby Bell, John Mackey, and Jackie Smith. The Steelers had no chance at any of them.

Parker quit during training camp in 1965 because Dan Rooney stepped in and quashed a deal that would have traded defensive linemen Ben McGee and Chuck Hinton to Philadelphia for quarterback King Hill. Parker felt he couldn't coach without autonomy and he walked away, just as he had in Detroit. Assistant Mike Nixon took over.

The Steelers last traded away their first-round draft choice in 1967. That cost them a chance at Hall of Famers Alan Page, Gene Upshaw, and Lem Barney. Since then they've made a couple of deals where they've switched positions in the first round, moving down in 2001 (Casey Hampton) and up in 2003 (Troy Polamalu) and 2006 (Santonio Holmes). But they haven't had a year where they've taken themselves out of the first round entirely.

That happened five times in Parker's eight years, and it obviously provided an example of how not to build a football team. Parker gave winning his best shot, with little concern for the future. The Steelers paid a steep price for his short-sightedness long after he'd left the team.

WHAT ARE THE TOP REASONS STEELERS FANS WILL MISS BILL COWHER?

Cowher resigned in January of 2007 after 15 years on the job, with one year left on his contract. That ended a relationship that started on January 21, 1992, when he replaced Chuck Noll.

It was a stormy ride at times. Until the Steelers beat Seattle in Super Bowl XL on February 5, 2006, Cowher was stuck with the label of being unable to win the big game. Prior to the 2005 season, he was 8–9 in the postseason, 1–4 in AFC championship games, and 0–1 in the Super Bowl.

But Steelers fans had unrealistically high expectations after Noll's teams went 4-for-4 in the Super Bowl in the 1970s. That was a different NFL, with no salary cap or free agency. Still, the bottom line remained the same: four championships in Noll's first 11 years on the job; in Cowher's first 13 years, no championships.

When Cowher finally won the Super Bowl, the accomplishment weighed in his decision to consider his work in Pittsburgh complete. Cowher moved to North Carolina in January 2007 to spend time with his family, also taking a part-time job with CBS. Mike Tomlin took over as Steelers head coach, and life is now different for both Cowher and the Steelers.

Here are the top reasons why things won't be the same without Cowher.

5. THE SWEATERS

Away from the sideline, Cowher was in the habit of wearing colorful sweaters that were undoubtedly selected by his wife. There were lots of bright hues in interesting patterns. If Hawaiians had any need for sweaters, they would have looked like the creations Cowher sported.

4. THE TUESDAY NEWS CONFERENCES

The Steelers have gotten so big over the years that there's live radio and TV coverage of the coach's mundane question-and-answer sessions. This gives fans a chance to not only critique the team, but to also pass judgment on the media's performance. Some of those fans watched too many Perry Mason reruns and apparently expected Cowher to fall into tears with an involuntary confession after being peppered with questions. But he was always in control, which often meant glaring and snapping off one-word answers to questions he didn't like. The sessions were rarely newsworthy, but they were often interesting television.

3. THE FACE

Some coaches stand dispassionately on the sideline, never letting their facial expression betray their thoughts. That was never an issue with Cowher. Nobody could snarl the way he did. His wide grin was the signal that things were going well. He once kissed quarterback Kordell Stewart on the sideline. When punter Josh Miller made a bad kick, Cowher would go into full rage, often losing his headset, cap, and sunglasses on the charge to confront Miller. Cowher's face would be contorted in a grimace, his jaw extended, and he'd spray spit as he shouted. Cowher's intensity was measured by the jut of that giant jaw. No one ever had to guess about Cowher's feelings.

2. THE TOUGHNESS

Cowher was a marginal NFL player as a backup linebacker and a special-teams demon. He lasted five years, mostly because of the work ethic and passion he brought. He never lost that edge after he retired. He demanded the same dedication from his players, and no team in the NFL played harder than the Steelers. Jerome Bettis plowed through tacklers with little regard for his own body; Hines Ward delivered devastating blocks; the defense made tackling a committee project. Cowher's Steelers never cheated anyone on effort.

1. THE RECORD

Cowher finished with a mark of 149–90–1 and the Steelers were in the playoffs in 10 of his 15 years. They only had three losing seasons. The team was consistently competitive despite the turnover created by roster and salary issues. Sure, another trip or two to the Super Bowl would have been great, but just look at how many coaches failed with other franchises during Cowher's fifteen seasons in Pittsburgh. Cowher's successor, Mike Tomlin, has a high standard to meet.

ARE THERE ANY MORE SUPER BOWL-ERA STEELERS WHO SHOULD BE IN THE HALL OF FAME?

17 The Steelers teams who won four Super Bowls from 1974 to 1979 almost have their own wing at the Hall of Fame in Canton, Ohio. Nine players from those teams have been inducted, along with coach Chuck Noll.

Two others have come close to making the cut—defensive end L. C. Greenwood has been a finalist, and safety Donnie Shell has also gotten serious consideration. So should either of them get the nod for a Hall selection?

Greenwood looked more like a basketball player, but his unconventional build (6 feet 8 inches and 245 pounds) helped him. He was quick and rangy enough to get past blockers. When he raised his long arms, he disrupted the quarterback's field of vision and sometimes batted down passes. Greenwood took a workmanlike approach to his job. His flash was in the gold high-top shoes he wore for games. He joined the Steelers as a tenth-round draft choice in 1969 and stayed through the 1981 season. He was credited with 73 and ½ sacks, which stood as the franchise record until linebacker Jason Gildon surpassed Greenwood in 2003. Greenwood made the Pro Bowl six times.

Shell came to training camp in 1974 as a free agent and was able to make a strong first impression while the veteran players were out on strike. Shell's fierce hits immediately pleased the coaching staff, and he won a roster spot. Shell played through 1987 and his 51 interceptions rank third on the Steelers' career list. Shell was in five Pro Bowls.

The problem with getting either player elected is that some voters believe the Steelers of that era have enough representation. Some voters who consider their candidacies marginal flatly reject them because they don't think the Steelers need any further recognition.

Greenwood was an integral part of the front four that harassed quarterbacks and completely shut down first-rate running games. He wasn't as dominant a player as Joe Greene was, but Greenwood was playing a different style at a different position. While he undoubtedly benefited from having Greene as a teammate, Greenwood was an exceptional force. He was consistently effective.

Some of Shell's biggest years came after the Super Bowl era. His longevity should be a factor, too, but his case isn't as strong as Greenwood's. He falls just short of Hall status, particularly on a team as talented as the Steelers of that era.

If voters have closed the doors to the Steelers of the 1970s, it's too bad. They missed one—L. C. Greenwood.

WAS THE SUPER BOWL XXX LOSS REALLY NEIL O'DONNELL'S FAULT?

18 The Steelers have played in six Super Bowls and won five of them. They lost Super Bowl XXX 27–17 to the Dallas Cowboys in Tempe, Arizona, on January 28, 1996, and every Steelers fan knows why. It was quarterback Neil O'Donnell's fault. Or was it?

O'Donnell had been one of the NFL's most efficient passers in the 1995 season, throwing just 7 interceptions on 416 pass attempts. But he threw 3 interceptions in the Super Bowl, two of them at critical points in the game.

It turned out to be his last game with the Steelers. O'Donnell was a free agent that off-season and signed a five-year, $25 million deal with the New York Jets. The fact that he never came back to Pittsburgh made it even easier to make him the villain for the Super Bowl loss. Despite his effective management of the Steelers offense en route to an 11–5 record and two playoff victories, O'Donnell was never a fan favorite. There were several reasons. First, Pittsburgh fans tend to blame the quarterback for any offensive failure. In addition, O'Donnell didn't have an especially appealing public profile. He was ultra-guarded with the media, limiting his availability during the week and speaking in clichés. Even a spot on the free-wheeling WDVE radio morning show failed to loosen his inhibitions.

There's no question that his Super Bowl interceptions were major factors in the loss to the Cowboys, a team the Steelers had beaten in two previous Super Bowls. But they weren't the only reason.

Dallas scored a touchdown and 2 field goals on its first 3 possessions, taking a 13–0 lead. That happened before O'Donnell threw a pass to the wrong team. The Steelers had a bad case of the jitters and were getting pushed off the ball. By the time the defense regained its poise, there was a 13-point deficit to overcome.

The interception that lives in infamy was the one with 4:15 left in the fourth quarter when the Steelers were trying to overcome a 20–17 deficit. Cornerback Larry Brown picked off the pass for his second interception of the game and returned it 33 yards to the Steelers' 6-yard line. Two plays later, Emmitt Smith ran 4 yards for a touchdown and the Cowboys put the game out of reach with 3:43 left. O'Donnell's fault? Partly. Receiver Andre Hastings was just as much to blame. He ran the wrong pattern and cut the wrong way. O'Donnell got the ball to the spot where Hastings was supposed to be. Hastings was in the wrong place. Although Hastings caught 10 passes for 98 yards, he made some other costly mistakes in the game. On an early series, he ran his pattern a yard short of the first-down marker and failed to sustain the drive. He later dropped a pass.

So was O'Donnell the reason for the Super Bowl loss? No. He had a bad game, but he had plenty of help in losing the game on that day.

WE ARE THE NON-CHAMPIONS

WHO WOULD MAKE THE STEELERS' ALL-TIME TEAM (NON-RING DIVISION)?

Picking the Steelers' all-time team shouldn't be too difficult. Nine of the players from the 1974–1979 Super Bowl champions are already in the Hall of Fame, so that's a good start.

But that's too easy, and it ignores the fact that the Steelers always had good players, even when they didn't have good teams. So let's disqualify anyone who has a Super Bowl ring from this team. That includes the stars of the 1970s, along with the players from the 2005 team who won Super Bowl XL. Let's dig a little deeper and find the best Steelers who never won a championship.

OFFENSE

19 WIDE RECEIVERS: LOUIS LIPPS (1984–1991) AND BUDDY DIAL (1959–1963)

Lipps was the Steelers' number-one draft choice in 1984, and wound up as the franchise's all-time number-3 pass catcher with 358 receptions. He trails only Hines Ward and

John Stallworth. Lipps is also third in receiving yards, with 6,016, and was a dangerous punt returner, too. He was selected for the Pro Bowl twice, even though the Steelers only reached the playoffs in four of his eight seasons.

Dial was originally drafted by the New York Giants. Despite playing only five years in Pittsburgh, he had 4,723 receiving yards and had a 235-yard game against Cleveland in 1961. The Steelers traded Dial to Dallas after the 1963 season to get the rights to defensive lineman Scott Appleton. Appleton signed with the AFL's Houston Oilers, and the Steelers had nothing to show for a trade that cost them their best receiver.

Honorable mention here goes to Roy Jefferson, Frank Lewis, and Jimmy Orr.

20 TIGHT END: ELBIE NICKEL (1947–1957)

A three-sport star at the University of Cincinnati, Nickel turned down a baseball contract from the Reds to play for the Steelers. He was adept at both catching passes and blocking, and helped define what the tight end position would become in the modern era of pro football. Nickel had 5,133 receiving yards, which remains a Steelers record for tight ends. The depth chart at this spot would have to include Eric Green and Gary Ballman.

21 TACKLES: FRANK VARRICHIONE (1955–1960) AND TUNCH ILKIN (1980–1992)

Varrichione was the team's number-one draft pick in 1955 and made the Pro Bowl five times in his career. Varrichione, who played at Notre Dame, once handled Baltimore's tough Gino Marchetti so well in 1957 that Cleveland coach Paul Brown used the game film as a tutorial for his offensive linemen. Ilkin arrived a year after the Steelers' Super Bowl run ended, but he had the opportunity to learn from the players on those teams. He made two Pro Bowl squads. He perfected a quick-strike blocking method called the "Tunch Punch" that was highlighted in a series of instructional videos. Who did these guys beat out? Charlie Bradshaw and Ted Doyle just miss the cut.

22 GUARDS: GEORGE HUGHES (1950–1954) AND MIKE SANDUSKY (1957–1965)

Hughes was the third pick in a very successful 1950 draft that produced Lynn Chadnois and Ernie Stautner on the first two rounds. Hughes had no intention of playing pro football until the Steelers' offer of $5,500 exceeded by $500 the amount he and his wife would have earned as teachers. He played 60 games without missing a start before he retired to start a hardware business. Hughes also punted and was part of the Steelers' goal line defense.

Sandusky overcame a serious leg injury in his youth to become a Pro Bowl player. Originally drafted by the San Francisco 49ers, Sandusky came to Pittsburgh in the same trade that brought quarterback Earl Morrall. He was a steady performer on the Steelers' line for nine seasons. Other worthy linemen who just miss the cut are John Nisby and Ray Lemek.

23 CENTER: DERMONTTI DAWSON (1988–2000)

Strong and quick, Dawson spent his rookie season playing guard alongside Hall of Fame center Mike Webster. The next year he took over at center and wound up starting 177 consecutive games at the position. A former track star, Dawson had the ability to lead the blocking on sweeps. "He did things no other center could do," coach Bill Cowher said. Dawson was named to seven Pro Bowls and was a semifinalist in his first year of eligibility for the Hall of Fame. Bill Walsh gets the nod as backup.

24 QUARTERBACK: BOBBY LAYNE (1958–1962)

When the Detroit Lions were willing to trade Layne, coach Buddy Parker picked him up in an instant. Layne rallied the Lions from a 16–10 deficit in the last three minutes to win the NFL championship for Parker in 1953. Layne came to Pittsburgh in 1958 and led the Steelers to two winning seasons in his four years. Brief as his career in Pittsburgh was, he's still the Steelers' fifth all-time passer with 8,983 passing yards, and ranks fourth in touchdown passes with 67. Layne got the Steelers to the second post-season game in their history, the 1962 playoff bowl. He said the biggest regret of his career was failing to win a championship for Art Rooney. Others quarterbacks to consider include Neil O'Donnell and Jim Finks.

RUNNING BACKS: BILL DUDLEY (1942, 1945–1946) AND JOHN HENRY JOHNSON (1960–1965)

The Pro Football Hall of Fame's official biography describes Dudley as "small and slow." So how did he get the nickname "Bullet"? Because he was always on the mark. In 1946, Dudley won the triple crown, leading the NFL in rushing, interceptions, and punt returns. He gained 8,217 combined yards in his career, with 478 points and 23 interceptions. Dudley was just 16 when he accepted a full scholarship to the University of Virginia. His Steelers career was cut short by conflict with coach Jock Sutherland, and he was subsequently traded to Detroit. Dudley was a member of the Hall of Fame class of 1966.

Johnson was drafted by the Steelers in 1953, but debuted in the NFL with San Francisco after a year in Canada. He was part of the 49ers "Million Dollar Backfield" with Y. A. Tittle, Hugh McElhenny, and Joe Perry.

Johnson ran 6,803 yards for 48 touchdowns and caught 186 passes for 1,478 yards and 7 touchdowns. He was also known as an exceptional blocker who often helped protect his quarterback. Johnson was inducted into the Hall of Fame in 1987.

Lynn Chadnois, Fran Rogel, Ray Mathews, and Tom "The Bomb" Tracy would back up this pair.

DEFENSE

26 ENDS: BILL McPEAK (1949–1957) AND BEN McGEE (1964–1972)

McPeak was a New Castle, Pennsylvania, native who was drafted from Pitt in the 14th round in 1949. He was an aggressive pass rusher who was also adept at stopping the inside running game. McGee was one of the few 1960s players who was able to stick around after Chuck Noll took over in 1969. McGee was big (6 feet 3 inches, 250 pounds) and rough with excellent speed. John Baker and Lou Michaels get honorable mention here.

27 TACKLES: ERNIE STAUTNER (1950–1963) AND EUGENE "BIG DADDY" LIPSCOMB (1962–1963)

Stautner is the greatest Steeler never to play on a championship team. He was undersized at 6 feet 1 inch, 230 pounds, but had freakish strength to go with quickness. Dan Rooney recalls a game against the New York Giants in which Stautner sacked the quarterback on three consecutive plays.

His toughness was legendary; Stautner missed only six games in his career. He was named to nine Pro Bowls and made the Hall of Fame in his first year of eligibility. Dick Hoak, who was with the Steelers for 45 years as a player and coach, said Stautner was, "pound for pound, mentally and physically, probably as tough a guy as I've ever seen."

Our other tackle, Eugene "Big Daddy" Lipscomb, played just two seasons with the Steelers before he was found dead from a drug overdose on May 20, 1963, at age 31. Lipscomb had played for the Rams and Colts before he came to the Steelers. At 6 feet 6 inches and 300 pounds, he was an intimidating pass rusher. Coach Buddy Parker called him "The best I ever saw at knocking people down."

Joel Steed, Joe Krupa, and Lloyd Voss are also worthy of mention at this spot.

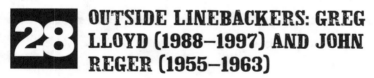

28 OUTSIDE LINEBACKERS: GREG LLOYD (1988–1997) AND JOHN REGER (1955–1963)

Lloyd was an emotional leader who constantly played in a fury. At one point the Steelers had an equipment helper assigned to reassemble Lloyd's helmet whenever the linebacker would smash it to the ground in frustration along the sidelines. His career was affected, however, by a serious knee injury sustained in the 1996 season opener.

Reger was a Pittsburgh native who quit football after his freshman year in college. He asked the Steelers for a tryout and won a spot on the roster. Known as "The Mighty Missile," the compactly built Reger made three Pro Bowls and was frequently the Steelers' leader in tackles.

Mike Merriweather, David Little, Jerry Shipkey, and Charlie Seabright are backups for these two linebacker picks.

29 MIDDLE LINEBACKER: DALE DODRILL (1951–1959)

Dodrill thought his football career would end after his years at Colorado A & M. Then he played in some all-star games and his plans changed. "I never figured I was as good as those guys from the East Coast that we read about all the time," he said. "I played in the all-star games and found I was as good as anyone else." Armed with that confidence, Dodrill joined the Steelers and made the Pro Bowl four times. He ended his career prematurely to get started in coaching. Myron Pottios and Hardy Nickerson deserve mention on the bench here.

30 CORNERBACKS: ROD WOODSON (1987–1996) AND JACK BUTLER (1951–1959)

Woodson was a superb athlete who could have played successfully on either side of the ball. After a prolonged holdout in his rookie season, he quickly established himself as one of the top players in the NFL. He was a seven-time Pro Bowl player with the Steelers. When a knee injury raised concerns about his ability to sustain a career, he was allowed to leave the team. He reinvented himself as a safety and played seven more seasons for three different teams

Butler was studying to become a priest and eschewing athletics at St. Bonaventure when he was asked to join the football team. The school's athletic director was Father Silas, the brother of Steelers founder Art Rooney Sr. After he made his way to the pro team, Butler gave the Steelers nine seasons, in which he intercepted 52 passes, including four in one game. His interception total is even more amazing because most teams designed game plans to avoid his side of the field. Butler's career was cut short by a knee injury.

Clendon Thomas, Brady Keys, and Dick Alban also merit consideration as cornerbacks.

 ## SAFETIES: CARNELL LAKE (1989–1998) AND DEAN DERBY (1957–1961)

Lake did everything for the Steelers, which included moving to cornerback when injuries created a need at that position. He was exceptional in coverage and he was also

a force as a pass rusher, collecting 18.5 sacks in his career with the Steelers. A lingering ankle injury and salary cap considerations ended his Pittsburgh career.

Derby was originally drafted by the Rams, but they traded him to the Steelers at the end of training camp that year. He was known for his speed and quick acceleration, which allowed him to keep up with receivers. Derby was also an analytical player who studied the tendencies of his opponents. That approach helped him develop a successful business career after he was finished with football.

Save backup spots at safety for Darren Perry, Marv Woodson, Tony Compagno, and Howard Hartley.

SPECIALISTS: GARY ANDERSON, KICKER (1982–1994), AND PAT BRADY, PUNTER (1952–1954)

Anderson was a steal as a waiver pickup from the Buffalo Bills. He owns most of the significant scoring and kicking records in Steelers history. The left-footed Brady was known for his booming kicks and still has the second-best career average (44.5 yards) in franchise history.

Mike Clark and Armand Niccolai are candidates at kicker, while Bobby Joe Green and Harry Newsome deserve mention as punters.

PIRATES
TREASURE

WERE THE 1979 PIRATES REALLY A "FAMILY"?

33
When Willie Stargell first heard Sister Sledge's "We Are Family," in 1979, he decided it was the perfect song for the Pirates.

The upbeat tune was played at home games, and the nation came to hear about it when the Pirates reached the postseason. As the first notes of "We Are Family" played during the National League playoffs, the wives of Pirates players abandoned their seats behind home plate at Three Rivers Stadium and got up on the roof of the dugout to dance. The gesture took even the players by surprise, but it cemented the relationship between that Pirates team and a song that had been on the Billboard Hot 100 chart for 19 weeks after debuting on April 29.

Joe L. Brown, who was general manager of the Pirates from 1956 to 1976, had always embraced and emphasized the idea of the Pirates as family. It was part of the speech he'd give to players when they first joined the team. Back then, there was no free agency, so players tended to stay with teams longer. The front office staff was small, typically fewer than 30 full-time employees. Because of the layout of the team offices at Forbes Field, the players often encountered most of the people who worked for the Pirates. It wasn't uncommon for the shortstop to be on a first-name basis with the accountant.

In 1979, it wasn't much different. Baseball was only four years into free agency and most of the signings were long term. There was still minimal movement from year to year, so bonds developed among the players. The Pirates had an added advantage with Stargell, who first came to the team in 1962.

Stargell was either 38 or 39 in 1979 (it was revealed after his death that he may have fudged his age by a year), but he was still a valid player. He appeared in 126 games, batting .281 with 32 home runs and 82 RBIs. That year Stargell shared the National League's Most Valuable Player award with Keith Hernandez of the St. Louis Cardinals. Credibility on the field added to his sway in the clubhouse. Despite chronically bad knees, Stargell played regularly.

The Pirates had some interesting and striking personalities in 1979. There were players everyone seemed to like (Bill Robinson, Phil Garner, Kent Tekulve) and those who hadn't fit in well with other teams (Tim Foli, Bill Madlock, John Milner). Respect for Stargell helped unify the Pirates.

It was Stargell who continued the "family" tradition that Brown had started. Stargell was the ultimate "people person" and a friend to everyone on the team, regardless of their status. Unlike some teams where the stars didn't mingle with role players, Stargell delighted in serving as a big brother to everyone on the roster. He had grown up in a collegial atmosphere with the Pirates, and he continued it. His ebullient personality made that natural. Stargell organized team parties on the road. He counseled anyone who wanted to talk. He handed out small gold stars that teammates proudly stuck on their caps. So when he called the Pirates a family, people bought the notion.

So, yes, the 1979 Pirates were a family—but no more so than the other Pirates teams of the 1970s, thanks to Willie Stargell.

WAS BARRY BONDS REALLY THAT BAD OF A GUY?

34 Has a great player ever been more unpopular with teammates and fans than Barry Bonds?

Bonds is a polarizing figure, one whose personality quirks would help author Jeff Pearlman fill 371 pages for the best-selling *Love Me, Hate Me: Barry Bonds and the Making of an Antihero* in 2006. We could talk about his antics for ages, but let's focus. This analysis is based solely on Bonds's first seven major league seasons, all spent with the Pirates.

He came to the major leagues for the first time in 1986 with a reputation as a tremendous talent, and as a guy who was often disliked by teammates. He lived up to his reputation on both counts.

Bonds won two Most Valuable Player awards with the Pirates (1990 and 1992) and just missed a third in 1991 when Atlanta's Terry Pendleton edged him out. The Pirates, who hadn't finished first since 1979, won three consecutive National League East titles with Bonds powering the lineup.

Since his father, Bobby, had played in the major leagues, Bonds grew up around the game and didn't have any of the rookie's usual sense of awe when he arrived. When Willie Mays is your godfather, you aren't intimidated by the group of last-place journeymen who made up the 1986 Pirates.

Teammates loved what Bonds did on the field, even if they didn't especially get along with him. And there were certainly clashes with teammates over the years. Bonds once fought with shortstop Jay Bell during a game. Bonds, batting leadoff, hit a foul pop that broke his bat. When the ball was caught, Bonds headed back to the dugout with the broken bat handle in his hand. He slammed it down in disgust. The splintered piece of wood bounced up and hit Bell, who was bent over to pick up his bat. Bell followed Bonds down the dugout tunnel and the two scuffled briefly until Pirates coaches broke it up.

Bonds had a famous showdown with manager Jim Leyland during spring training of 1992. Bonds was upset that a photographer was on the field, and wound up arguing with coach Bill Virdon. Leyland jumped in, and the one-sided, nose-to-nose confrontation was an endless bleep-fest when it was shown on television. Although fans loved the way Leyland stood up to Bonds, Leyland wanted the episode to go away after it had been settled. When spring training crowds loudly booed Bonds, Leyland used the media to ask fans to knock it off.

Bonds consistently made himself available to the media, although the level of his cooperation varied wildly. In 1992, for example, Bonds got off to a slow start. After one Saturday night game, two sportswriters were standing in the clubhouse, waiting for the starting pitcher to emerge from the trainers' room. Bonds called to them. "You guys want something to write? Write about how bad I am and how I'm messing everything up for this team." Bonds did a ten-minute confessional about his slow start, and the writers no longer had an interest in the starting pitcher.

But you had to get Bonds when the mood was right. Shortly after his first child was born, Bonds regaled a couple of reporters with a sensitive account of how fatherhood had changed his life for the better. He said he couldn't get home quickly enough after games to hold the baby, and told how he would sometimes sit for hours, just watching his infant son sleep. A few weeks later an out-of-town writer came in to do a feature on Bonds. Someone suggested he pursue the fatherhood angle. When the writer asked how being a father had changed him, Bonds dismissed the subject abruptly with, "Wakes me up at night."

The simple act of signing autographs could bring out both sides of Bonds as well. During the 1992 season, Major League Baseball undertook a project to get an All-Star game program autographed by every player who had been on the roster. Someone from the commissioner's office would hand off the program to the public relations directors when their teams visited New York. Pirates publicist Jim Trdinich picked up the program and explained the project to Andy Van Slyke, who signed on the designated spot. Trdinich turned and started to explain the process to Bonds, only to look up and see Bonds's middle finger just a few inches away. He took that as a signal Bonds wasn't going to sign.

There was a completely different autograph story later that season. A man in a wheelchair regularly stationed himself outside the press gate at Three Rivers Stadium, trying to get autographs. He had a large binder filled with cards and photos. At one time or another, each player stopped and signed for him. His problem was that some players didn't enter the park through that gate. They would come in through the Pirates' offices, which were on the other side of the stadium.

One day Bonds was spotted quietly circulating through

the clubhouse with the binder, getting teammates to sign the pictures. He didn't do it for show, but had simply brought the man's material into the clubhouse, collecting the signatures the fan had missed.

These stories are the essence of Barry Bonds's demeanor in his time with the Pirates. The verdict? Bonds seems more erratic than evil.

WHAT WAS THE BIGGEST BREAK THE PIRATES GOT IN THE 1960 WORLD SERIES?

 What do you call a team that loses three World Series games by embarrassing scores of 16–3, 12–0, and 10–0? The World Champion Pittsburgh Pirates.

They were blown out in three games and won four close ones. According to shortstop Dick Groat, that's all the critics of the 1960 Pirates need to know. When the games were close, the Pirates found a way to win.

The Pirates' 10–9 win in the seventh game was one of the wildest in World Series history and featured two points in the eighth inning that turned things in

Pittsburgh's favor. The most obvious was Bill Virdon's possible double-play grounder that hit a pebble, took a bad hop, and struck Yankees shortstop Tony Kubek in the throat. That allowed the Pirates to sustain a rally that would have otherwise died.

Following that, though, Yankees reliever Jim Coates got two outs with two runners on base, and it looked as though he was about to escape the jam. But then came the second turning point, as Roberto Clemente hit a dribbler between the pitcher's mound and first base. Coates was late covering the base, and Clemente wound up with a single.

The first drills of spring training every year are PFP—baseball shorthand for pitchers' fielding practice. They spend hours practicing the simple art of covering first base when a ball is hit on the right side of the infield. But that fundamental escaped Coates on the last game of the series, and the Pirates made him pay. The next hitter, Hal Smith, blasted a 3-run homer that gave the Pirates a temporary 9–7 lead.

Maybe the World Series was swayed before it even started. After all, it's traditional for a team to use its best starter in the first game. That means he can pitch three times if the Series goes seven games. Yet Yankees manager Casey Stengel started Art Ditmar in the first game and didn't use ace Whitey Ford until the third game. Ditmar led the Yankees that year with fifteen victories while Ford had twelve, but the unflappable Ford was considered a big-game pitcher who had extensive World Series experience. Twenty-five years after that World Series, Yogi Berra was still wondering why Stengel didn't make Ford the number-one starter. That question became more valid after Ford handled the Pirates with ease in his two starts: He pitched 2 shutouts in games 3 and 6 and held the Pirates to just 11 hits over the 18 innings. Meanwhile, Ditmar was knocked out in the 1st and 2nd innings of his starts. He was the losing pitcher in both and had a Series ERA of 21.60.

While Stengel's decision was curious, the Pirates' biggest break was Coates's mental mistake. The bad hop grounder was a random occurrence; Coates's failure to cover first base was the kind of error a team as professional and experienced as the Yankees wasn't supposed to make.

WHY DID THE PIRATES RETIRE BILLY MEYER'S NUMBER? SHOULD THEY HAVE DONE SO?

If you look over the list of eight players whose numbers have been retired by the Pirates, most of them need no introduction.

We can start with Honus Wagner (No. 33), Roberto Clemente (No. 21), and Willie Stargell (No. 8), all of whom are honored with statues on the sidewalks outside of PNC Park. Ralph Kiner (No. 4) is saluted with a display inside the left-field entrance. A street outside the park is named for Bill Mazeroski (No. 9). There's also Pie Traynor (No. 20), who played for the Pirates, managed the team, then enjoyed a second career on radio and television in Pittsburgh. Danny Murtaugh (No. 40) is the only manager to lead the Pirates to two World Series titles.

Then there's Billy Meyer and his No. 1. Meyer managed the Pirates from 1948 to 1952, a time in which they had one winning season. His first team was 83–71 and finished fourth in the eight-team National League. His last team lost 112 games, which is still a Pirates record, just as the .273 winning percentage is the worst in the Pirates' 121 seasons.

Meyer played in the major leagues, but his career was brief and confined to the Chicago White Sox and Philadelphia Athletics. Yet the Pirates retired his number in 1954, at a time when only Wagner had been given that distinction. Why?

Meyer's retired number is a matter of emotion overruling merit. He was in poor health for much of his time as Pirates manager and died in 1957 at the age of 65. He had great rapport with his players and the press, so the Pirates decided to give him a tribute. Instead of having an appreciation day for him, they went overboard and retired his number.

After making a mistake with Meyer, the Pirates became a little stingy about the honor. Traynor's No. 20 remained in circulation until 1972, when the Pirates took it off Richie Hebner. Clemente (1973) and Murtaugh (1977) had their numbers retired immediately after their deaths. Stargell's number was retired after his final game in 1982 and brought back when he rejoined the team as a coach two years later. Kiner and Mazeroski were given their overdue recognition as part of the franchise's 100th anniversary celebration in 1987.

The most glaring omissions from the list of retired numbers were brothers Paul and Lloyd Waner, who wore

Nos. 11 and 10 for the Pirates in the 1940s. Paul "Big Poison" Waner had a lifetime average of .333, drove in 1,309 runs, and was elected to the Hall of Fame in 1952. Lloyd "Little Poison" Waner batted .316 in his career and was enshrined in the Hall in 1967.

Their numbers have been worn by a succession of nondescript players (No. 10 has been sported by Ken Reitz, Benny Distefano, and Johnnie LeMaster, while Mario Mendoza, Kurt Bevacqua, and Mike Kingery have worn No. 11). The Pirates finally got it right and retired No. 10 in a ceremony during the 2007 season.

Meanwhile, the number of a manager whose winning percentage was .412 is retired—all because of overzealous goodwill.

HOW DID THE PIRATES GO FROM POWERHOUSE TO LAUGHINGSTOCK?

In October of 1992, the Pirates were one pitch away from the World Series. Three years later they were in danger of leaving town.

The rapid transition happened for several reasons. Ownership either didn't have enough money, or was reluctant to spend it. Major League Baseball's botched labor strategy was a key factor. The Pirates also did a poor job of running their organization.

The Pirates understood that 1992 was their last opportunity to contend for a while. Before the season they lost cleanup hitter Bobby Bonilla to free agency and 20-game-winner John Smiley to a financially motivated trade, and they were due to lose two other cornerstones after 1992. Barry Bonds and pitcher Doug Drabek were both eligible for free agency, and the Pirates didn't make a serious offer to either player. With all of this hanging over the team's head, they managed to get off to a hot start (21–8 through May 8). That, combined with a mediocre division, helped the Pirates win their third straight National League East title.

After the failure to make the World Series, ownership's strategy was to rebuild and wait for the 1994 labor show-down that was expected to be resolved with a salary cap. Inexpensive minor league players were brought up, and the Pirates girded for the strike they thought would bring financial equity. The 1994 season ended in early August, and Major League Baseball (MLB) took the unprecedented step of canceling the World Series. As replacement players were set to open the 1995 season, a court decision pushed MLB into essentially the same labor contract that had been in place. Pirates ownership, a consortium of public and private interests, put the team up for sale and minimized its financial commitment: they short-changed scouting and player development while also cutting the major league payroll wherever possible.

Kevin McClatchy, a 33-year-old newspaper heir, put together a group to buy the franchise, and MLB pulled some strings to approve the sale to a group it knew was undercapitalized, by commissioner Bud Selig's admission. Why? MLB was anxious to keep the Pirates in Pittsburgh. It believed a new ballpark would allow the Pirates to compete because it would generate more revenue, allowing the franchise to hold on to its best young players. The salvation of the Pirates would be this publicly funded baseball-only park, guaranteed to open by 2001.

But the young talent never really developed, and the Pirates wasted their money on mediocre free agents such as Pat Meares and Derek Bell. Instead of blossoming into a winner in 2001, the Pirates lost one hundred games, feuded with their fans over the issue of bringing food and drink into the new ballpark, then followed that public relations gaffe by raising ticket prices.

Because the organization had not built a good player development system, the losing continued through three changes of managers. The Pirates threw away more money trying to patch holes with short-term veterans. An unexpected in-season money shortfall led the Pirates to give away Aramis Ramirez, the franchise's only homegrown power hitter. Meanwhile, the obsession with ending a streak of losing seasons led them to sign more borderline veterans to take a run at being respectable. That plan failed.

While MLB's economic system is the most obvious enemy of franchises in smaller markets, the Pirates' own neglect and ineptitude have created the longest losing streak in the franchise's 121-year history.

WHO'S THE BETTER PLAYER: DAVE PARKER OR BRIAN GILES?

 Dave Parker looked like he was headed to the Hall of Fame in the mid-1970s. He was the best player in baseball, a fearsome combination of finesse and power who was big enough to play tight end in the NFL.

Meanwhile, when Brian Giles came over from Cleveland in a trade following the 1998 season, first impressions were underwhelming. Giles had a squatty blacksmith's build and looked like a clone of Lenny Dykstra, the Philadelphia Phillies' center fielder.

Parker was homegrown, drafted by the Pirates in the 14th round out of Cincinnati's Courter Tech High School. He injured a knee playing football in his senior year, which scared some teams away from drafting him. Parker's progress through the Pirates' farm system was slow, blocked by excellence at the major league level. Willie Stargell was still playing left field, Al Oliver was in center, and Richie Zisk claimed right field following Roberto Clemente's death. Parker spent parts of the 1973 and 1974 seasons on the Pirates bench before he forced his way into the lineup. Zisk moved to left field, Stargell went to first base, and Parker took over in right field. In 1975, his first as a regular, he batted .308 with 25 home runs and 101 runs batted in. His breakthrough season was 1977, when he won the National League batting title with a .338 average. The next year he hit .334 with 30 home runs and 117 RBIs to win the Most Valuable Player award. His timing was perfect. Parker was eligible for free agency and the Pirates gave him a five-year contract that, with some incentives, could pay him up to $1 million per year. It was a groundbreaking contract, and was also the start of Parker's problems with the Pirates.

He allowed himself to get grossly out of shape, which led to a succession of injuries. He hit .295 in 1980, his best average in his last four seasons with the Pirates. He became a lightning rod for fan discord, which culminated with someone from the stands throwing a bat in his direction on Bat Day at Three Rivers Stadium in 1980. Parker's Pittsburgh career ended with a whimper in 1983. His numbers that season were ordinary: .279 average, 12 home runs, and 69 RBIs.

Giles was considered expendable by the Indians because they had a surplus of young bats and needed some help for their bullpen. They traded Giles to the Pirates for left-handed pitcher Ricardo Rincon, a situational reliever who was usually called upon to face especially tough left-handed batters. Everything about Giles's time in Pittsburgh was positive. He was a consistent producer, even though the Pirates' lineups were rarely strong. In four full seasons, Giles hit at least 35 home runs every year and never batted lower than .298. His OPS, a combination of slugging percentage and on-base average, never dipped below .994. Giles was a rare power hitter who also had uncommon plate discipline.

Giles's arm was never close to Parker's—one of Parker's best assets was his powerful throwing arm. He threw out runners at third base and home plate in the 1979 All-Star game to take MVP honors. But Giles was an underrated defensive player who adjusted to covering the abnormally large left field in PNC Park. Put aside the throwing, and he was Parker's equal as a defensive player.

Parker rose and fell with the Pirates from 1973 to 1983. Giles provided machine-like consistency in his four and a half years in Pittsburgh. That reliability trumps Parker's great seasons of 1978 and 1979 and makes Giles the clear choice in this showdown.

WHICH PIRATES MANAGER HAD THE MOST UNUSUAL CAREER?

39 Danny Murtaugh managed the Pirates for 2,065 games, second only to George Clarke's 2,391 on the Pirates' career list.

Clarke was in charge from 1900 to 1915, but Murtaugh's managerial career covered three different decades in four different terms. Until George Steinbrenner started bringing back Billy Martin every other year, Murtaugh held the major league record for the most different stints managing the same team.

He first got the job on August 3, 1957, when he was promoted from the coaching staff to replace Bobby Bragan. General manager Joe L. Brown, who had worked with Murtaugh in the minor leagues, made the move after he felt Bragan had embarrassed the organization during a confrontation with an umpire. Murtaugh was 39 when he took over as manager. The Pirates were contenders in 1958 and won the World Series in 1960. Murtaugh stayed through the 1964 season, stepping down because of health concerns. He then moved into a front office role, advising Brown on player personnel.

Murtaugh returned to managing when Harry Walker was fired midway through the 1967 season. He finished the season with a 39–39 record, unable to rally a team that was supposed to be a contender. The players knew Murtaugh was there on an interim basis and had little motivation to shake the bad habits they'd developed under Walker's watch.

Murtaugh's next two returns were surprising. The Pirates fired manager Larry Shepard at the end of the 1969 season and were considering a number of candidates when Murtaugh called Brown and told him he was interested in the job. Murtaugh had been given a clean bill of health by his doctors and the blessing of his wife, Katie. When Murtaugh announced his availability, Brown no longer had a tough decision. Murtaugh had an obvious reason for wanting to return. He had been evaluating the talent in the Pirates' system and knew there was an amazing abundance of good players ready to establish themselves in the major leagues. The list included Al Oliver, Manny Sanguillen, Richie Hebner, Dave Cash, Bob Robertson, Dock Ellis, Bob Moose, Gene Clines, and Milt May. He was right—the Pirates won the National League East in 1970, then took the World Series in 1971. That victory allowed Murtaugh to retire as a winner. His hand-picked successor, Bill Virdon, took over and led the team to another National League East title.

But the 1973 season was filled with turmoil. Roberto

Clemente had been killed in a New Year's Eve 1972 plane crash, and the team's number-one starting pitcher, Steve Blass, had inexplicably lost the pinpoint control that made him a 19-game winner in 1972. Virdon had an ugly clubhouse confrontation with Hebner during the season and Brown became convinced Virdon had lost the club. Although the Pirates were tied for second place, just three games behind first-place St. Louis, on September 6 Brown fired Virdon and asked Murtaugh to come back.

After some reluctance, Murtaugh agreed. Brown had convinced him a managerial change was in the best interests of the organization. Mindful of what had happened in 1967 when Murtaugh was on hand as a caretaker, Brown emphasized that Murtaugh had also signed to manage the team in 1974. The Pirates, 67–69 when the change was made, were just 13–13 under Murtaugh and finished third, 2 1/2 games behind the New York Mets.

The 1974 season started terribly, with the Pirates in last place at 18–32 on June 7. But a July 14 fight with the Cincinnati Reds seemed to invigorate the Pirates. They went on a 54–22 streak to end the season and won the National League East. The strong finish also energized Murtaugh, who signed on to return. The Pirates won their division in 1975, a season that had its share of turmoil. Murtaugh battled some disgruntled players, with Dock Ellis leading the charge. Ellis was suspended for insubordination and Murtaugh's famously peaceful clubhouse atmosphere was rocked by the clash. Ellis was traded after the season and Murtaugh returned, yet again, for the 1976 season. But the Pirates' late charge fell short and the Philadelphia Phillies won the division. In the last week of the season, Murtaugh and Brown separately announced their intentions to step down after the season. Murtaugh revealed that he had experienced health problems during the season ("I was sick more times than anyone knew") and said he was looking forward to a less stressful life, enjoying his grandchildren and helping the Pirates' front office. He never had the chance to follow through on those plans. Murtaugh suffered a stroke in late November and died on December 2, 1976, two months and a day after he'd managed his last game.

His four terms as manager were testimony to Brown's belief that he was the best manager in the game. Twice Brown called on him to rescue seasons that had gone awry. Brown hired three other men to manage the Pirates during his years as general manager. He replaced every one of them with Danny Murtaugh.

WHO'S BETTER: ROBERTO CLEMENTE OR BARRY BONDS?

 Ah, if this could be settled with sentiment, there would be no need to carry the debate past this paragraph.

Clemente was the Pirates' sainted right fielder from 1955 to 1972, and died a hero's death on December 31, 1972, when his plane crashed while delivering relief supplies to earthquake victims in Nicaragua. Bonds was the supremely talented left fielder from 1986 to 1992, who wasn't popular with fans or teammates, despite playing at a level that virtually guaranteed he would match Clemente's Hall of Fame status.

Comparing players from different eras is difficult. Clemente was among the first generation of Latin American players who encountered significant obstacles off the field. Major League Baseball wasn't even fully integrated until 1959, which was Clemente's fifth season in the major leagues. From a baseball standpoint, when Clemente first played for Pittsburgh, the National League had eight teams and no franchise west of St. Louis. Clemente played the bulk of his home games in asymmetrical Forbes Field. During 14 of his 17 seasons, pitchers worked from a mound that was 15 inches high. The mound was lowered to ten inches after a pitching-dominated 1968 season because the higher mound was believed to give the pitchers an advantage with increased leverage.

Bonds was the son of major league player Bobby Bonds, and his godfather was Willie Mays. He grew up around the game, so any sense of awe he had at reaching the major leagues was likely minimal. Where Clemente prepped for the major leagues with one minor league season, Bonds came from a high-powered baseball program at Arizona State University, then advanced through the Pirates' minor league system in just over a year.

Bonds's career has come in an era with six more major league franchises than existed in Clemente's day. Bonds's time has also included interleague play, video scouting, and advanced methods of training and nutrition.

So how can we compare? Let's do it the baseball way. Baseball scouts have long had a way to cut through the clutter of evaluation, ranking position players in five "tool" categories. Here's a look at Clemente vs. Bonds.

BATTING AVERAGE

This is mostly a wash. Clemente batted .317 in his career and Bonds headed into the 2007 season with a .299 career average. Bonds is still playing at age 43, though, and his game has declined, taking points off his average.

Clemente was 38 in his final season and batted .352, .341, and .312 in his last three seasons. Call this one even.

HITTING FOR POWER

Clemente's biggest home run season saw him hit 29 in 1966, which was tenth in the National League. He never ranked higher than tenth in home runs. Of course, he also played in Forbes Field, which was 365 feet to left field, 406 to left center, 457 to the deepest part of left center, and 435 to center. Even the right-center field gap was 408 feet from home plate. Home runs were not cheap at Forbes Field for right-handed hitters. Still, Clemente ranked in the top 10 in slugging percentage six times in 17 years, one of which came after the Pirates had moved to Three Rivers Stadium. He was in the top 10 for total bases five times.

Even before Bonds suspiciously bulked up, he was a consistent home run hitter, albeit in Three Rivers, which had standard dimensions. Bonds's homer totals have increased along with his jersey size, and he set baseball's all-time home-run record in 2007, besting Henry Aaron. Putting the issue of his workout plan aside, Bonds was a formidable power hitter even before he got bigger, and he gets the edge in this category.

SPEED

Clemente stole 83 bases in his career. Bonds had 52 in one season, 1990, with the Pirates. That alone doesn't decide the issue, though, because the strategy of attempting steals changed over the years. Very few players of Clemente's era had permission to run on their own. Baseball protocol was different then, too, and stolen base attempts were much more limited. Still, Clemente was fast, but the young Bonds could fly. Edge to Bonds.

ARM STRENGTH

This is no contest. At his absolute best, Bonds maybe had an average arm. Clemente made throws that appeared to be launched from a cannon. Huge edge to Clemente.

FIELDING ABILITY

Clemente gets the anecdotal edge, certainly. Stories of catches he made are legendary. But Bonds is no slouch. Even though Bonds played left field, which is often considered a hiding place for defensively inferior players, he was an outstanding fielder. The flashiness factor comes into play here —Clemente played with a great flair, while Bonds made most plays look easy. Bonds's defense wasn't fully appreciated until he left and everyone saw all the balls that Al Martin didn't get to in left field. Bonds won eight Gold Glove awards; Clemente won 12. Bonds won his last at age 34; Clemente's final award came in his last season. Edge to Clemente.

Each player claims two categories with one tie. So what's the tiebreaker? It's twofold.

First, there's the postseason. Clemente played in five series and flopped in only one. He had a single in 14 at-bats during the 1970 National League playoffs against Cincinnati. Take that away and he batted .355 in the post-season (two playoffs and two World Series). He hit safely in all 14 of his World Series games and led the Pirates to their victory over Baltimore in the 1971 World Series.

Bonds came into 2007 with a .245 overall postseason average. His breakthrough didn't come until 2002, when he batted .471 with 4 home runs and 6 runs batted in against Anaheim in the World Series. Before that year he'd been in five postseason series and hit .196 with 1 home run and 6 RBIs in 97 at-bats. Clearly, Clemente was the better player in the biggest games.

There is also the unavoidable issue of Bonds's possible use of performance-enhancing substances after his career moved to San Francisco. There is much circumstantial evidence, including the abnormally thick muscles he developed late in his career. If Bonds's career is tainted by those suspicions, it's both a shame and his own fault. Bonds was established as one of the premier players in baseball before he added muscle and probably would have continued on that career course. But his weight gain, accompanied by suddenly monstrous power numbers, put his career accomplishments in a different light.

No question Bonds is one of the greatest talents in the history of baseball. But with so many of his accomplishments possibly tainted, the choice has to be Clemente. He didn't achieve as much, but he did it without artificial assistance.

WHAT WERE THE PIRATES' FIVE BEST TRADES?

41 Trading players probably started about 5 minutes after the first organized baseball league began operations. Teams are always looking to improve, and they always covet players on other teams. Until free agency came along in 1976, trading was the only way to add experienced talent. Fans thrived on off-season trade rumors as teams tried to fill needs by dealing from a surplus.

So what were the Pirates' best trades? For the purposes of this argument, the best trades are being identified as those that brought back significant talent at a modest price. Special consideration is also given to trades that helped win championships or, at the very least, enhanced the Pirates' status as a contender.

5. GRIMES'S PRIME TIME

Burleigh Grimes from the New York Giants for pitcher Vic Aldridge, February 11, 1928

Grimes was the game's last legal spitball pitcher. The pitch was banned in 1920, but he was one of 17 pitchers who were grandfathered in and allowed to continue to use their specialty. Grimes started his career with the Pirates in 1916 and lasted two seasons before he was traded to Brooklyn in a six-player deal that brought Casey Stengel to Pittsburgh. The Pirates got Grimes back and were rewarded with seasons in which he was 25–14 and 17–7. The cost to get him was Aldridge, who lasted less than one full season with the Giants before he retired. Grimes left the Pirates after two years in a contract dispute.

4. SETTLING CENTER FIELD

Outfielder Bill Virdon from the St. Louis Cardinals for outfielder Bobby Del Greco and pitcher Dick Littlefield, May 17, 1956

Impulsive Cardinals general manager Frank Lane gave up too soon on Virdon, who was hitting just .211 at the time of the trade. It turned into a steal for the Pirates. Del Greco was a good fielding but light-hitting outfielder who batted just .215 for the Cardinals in 102 games. He went on to play part time for four other teams. Littlefield pitched three games for the Cardinals before he was traded to the New York Giants in a nine-player deal. Meanwhile, Virdon settled in for a ten-year run as Pittsburgh's center fielder and lead-off hitter. He was durable, averaging 142 games over his career with the Pirates, and posting an overall .267 average in those years. Virdon could have played several more years, but chose to retire at age 34 after the 1965 season to begin a managerial career.

3 BULLPEN BARGAIN

Pitcher Dave Giusti and catcher Dave Ricketts from the St. Louis Cardinals for catcher and first baseman Carl Taylor and outfielder Frank Vanzin, October 21, 1969

The Pirates miscalculated on this deal, because they thought Giusti could help their starting rotation. His failure to land a starting spot sent him to the bullpen, where he emerged as the closer for the teams that won three straight National League East titles from 1970 to 1972. Giusti was 21–13 with a 2.70 earned run average in those seasons and posted 78 saves. Unlike today's closers, Giusti often pitched more than 1 inning for his saves. In those three years, 78 of his 128 appearances (61 percent) were for more than 1 inning. Ricketts was strictly a backup catcher, but turned out to be such a positive clubhouse influence that the Pirates hired him as a coach after taking him off the roster. Taylor was a utility player who had no set position. He hit .348 for the Pirates in a part-time role in 1969. In 104 games with the 1970 Cardinals, he batted .249 with 6 home runs and 45 runs batted in. He never had more than 145 major league at-bats in any season after 1970 and wound up coming back to the Pirates briefly in 1971. Vanzin never played in the major leagues.

2. LAST PIECES IN PLACE

Pitcher Harvey Haddix, catcher Smoky Burgess, and third baseman Don Hoak from the Cincinnati Reds for outfielder Frank Thomas, pitcher Whammy Douglas, and outfielders Jim Pendleton and John Powers, January 30, 1959

This was the deal that helped put the Pirates over the top for their march to the 1960 World Series title. General manager Joe L. Brown gave up one quality player (Thomas) and got three solid major leaguers to add to a homegrown core of talent. Haddix was the left-handed complement to Vernon Law and Bob Friend in the starting rotation, and won two games in the 1960 Series. Burgess was a natural hitter who was a platoon partner of Hal Smith behind the plate. The fiery Hoak was an inspirational leader who plugged the hole at third base left by Thomas's departure. The Pirates got three good seasons from Haddix and Hoak and four from Burgess, who never hit below .294 with Pittsburgh. Thomas hit 12 home runs in his one year with the Reds after getting 161 homers in six seasons with the Pirates. Douglas never returned to the major leagues. Pendleton hit .257 in 113 at-bats with the Reds, then didn't return to the majors until he played for the expansion Houston Colt 45s in 1962. Powers had 43 at-bats for the Reds in 1959, his last full season in the major leagues.

1. BARGAIN POWER SURGE

Outfielder Brian Giles from the Cleveland Indians for pitcher Ricardo Rincon, November 18, 1998

General manager Cam Bonifay didn't do a lot of things right in his eight years on the job, but this was his major achievement. Giles was the Pirates best player from 1999 to 2003, and the price to get him was a very expendable left-handed reliever. The Indians had a surplus of outfielders and Giles wasn't about to displace Manny Ramirez, Kenny Lofton, Dave Justice, or Mark Whiten. That made him viable trade bait for the situational lefty the contending Indians felt they needed for the bullpen. Giles was in the National League's top ten for on-base percentage in every year he spent with the Pirates, and ranked among the top ten in OPS (on-base percentage plus slugging percentage) every year, too. His average was .320 and he also averaged 37 home runs, 109 RBIs, and 108 runs every season as well. The Pirates never had a winning season during Giles's stay, but that wasn't his fault. He posted Hall-of-Fame-level numbers in his years with the Pirates. Why is this trade the best? The Pirates have never gotten such a good player at such a modest cost.

WHAT WERE THE PIRATES' FIVE WORST TRADES?

The other side of the coin is those regrettable deals, the kind where a team gives up a Brian-Giles-like talent and gets so little in return.

One disclaimer: In recent years, the Pirates have made trades motivated primarily by finances. In their haste to unload a contract, they've made trades that bring back virtually nothing. Those kinds of deals are excluded here. So while trading third baseman Aramis Ramirez to the Chicago Cubs for nothing was an abjectly horrible deal, we'll leave it off the table. The Pirates knew they were getting nothing but payroll relief when they signed off on the Ramirez trade. We're talking about the worst of the worst here: deals in which the Pirates thought they were getting something back, and wound up hugely disappointed.

5. CUYLER GIVEAWAY

Outfielder Kiki Cuyler to the Chicago Cubs for infielder Sparky Adams and outfielder Pete Scott, 1927

Cuyler had been the hero of the 1925 World Series when his bases-clearing double off Washington's Walter Johnson clinched the title for the Pirates. Two years later Cuyler was on the bench and didn't even appear in the 1927 Series against the Yankees. He clashed with manager Donie Bush and infuriated owner Barney Dreyfuss with a salary dispute, so Cuyler's ticket out of town was punched. Despite hitting over .300 in every full season he spent with the Pirates, he was dealt for two journeyman players. Adams had two decent seasons for the Pirates before he was sold to the Cardinals. Scott's major league career ended with the 60 games he played for the Pirates in 1928. Cuyler went on to six more seasons in which he hit over .300. He wound up with a career average of .321 and was elected to the Hall of Fame in 1968. Maybe the Pirates had to deal Cuyler, but they should have gotten more for a player of his stature.

4. DOCTOR'S HOUSE CALL DOESN'T HELP

Second baseman Willie Randolph and pitchers Dock Ellis and Ken Brett to the New York Yankees for pitcher George "Doc" Medich, 1975

The Pirates were having attendance problems, so the idea of bringing Aliquippa, Pennsylvania, native (and University of Pittsburgh medical student) Medich home was appealing. He had also been a reliable pitcher for the Yankees and appeared to be heading toward his prime years at age 27. Medich's only season in Pittsburgh was a disappointment as he went 8–11 with a 3.52 ERA in 29 games. It was one of two losing seasons he would have in an 11-year major league career. The Pirates knew Randolph was a top prospect, but they felt they were set at second base with Rennie Stennett. Randolph was the Yankees' regular second baseman for 12 years and ranked among the American League's top ten in on-base percentage six times. The Pirates were forced to trade Ellis because of his run-ins with manager Danny Murtaugh during the 1975 season. Joe L. Brown predicted a big year for Ellis in New York, and he was correct: Ellis was 17–8 with a 3.19 ERA and won a game in the playoffs, too. By the next season, he'd worn out his welcome in New York and was traded to Oakland for Mike Torrez. The oft-injured Brett was a throw-in who appeared in just two games for the Yankees before he was dealt to the Chicago White Sox.

3. REGRETTABLE REDS PITCHER

Bob Purkey to the Cincinnati Reds for pitcher Don Gross, 1957

When Joe L. Brown retired as general manager at the end of the 1976 season, he picked this deal as his worst. It was a straight trade of right-handed pitchers that the Reds won by a huge margin. Gross pitched in 40 games for the Pirates in 1958, then appeared in just 26 games over the next two seasons. He was 6–8 with a 3.82 ERA. Purkey became Cincinnati's staff leader, averaging 227 innings per season for seven years. He was 103–76 for the Reds with a 3.50 ERA and helped them get to the 1961 World Series. Purkey was 23–5 in 1962 and also had two seasons with 17 victories. He often reminded the Pirates of their mistake: He was 16–8 against Pittsburgh with a 2.99 ERA. Roberto Clemente considered Purkey one of the toughest pitchers he faced. In 94 career plate appearances against Purkey, Clemente batted just .195 with no home runs and 11 RBIs.

2. ONE YEAR BROWN OUT
Pitcher Jon Lieber to the Chicago Cubs for outfielder Brant Brown, 1998

This was Cam Bonifay at his worst. He took the advice of assistant general manager Roy Smith, who assured him that Brown could plug the hole in center field the Pirates had since Andy Van Slyke left after the 1994 season. The evaluation was badly misguided. Brown hit .232 with 16 home runs and 58 RBIs in his only season with the Pirates. He struck out 114 times in 341 at-bats and his defense was poor. Lieber, 28 years old when he was traded, became a key part of the Cubs' rotation and went 20–6 in 2001, finishing fourth in the Cy Young Award voting. By then Brown was a distant memory with the Pirates, having been traded to Florida for Bruce Aven just one year after the Pirates had acquired him.

1. A GIANT MISTAKE

Pitcher Jason Schmidt and outfielder John Vander Wal to the San Francisco Giants for pitcher Ryan Vogelsong and outfielder Armando Rios, 2001

This was Dave Littlefield's first trade and it set the unfortunate tone for his tenure as general manager. Schmidt was nearing free agency and had no interest in staying in Pittsburgh, so he had to go. The Pirates determined that Vogelsong would be an adequate replacement. The swap of fourth outfielders was considered even. Schmidt became the anchor of the Giants' staff. In five and half seasons with the Giants, he was 78–37 with a 3.36 ERA. He was also 3–1 in the postseason with a 3.06 ERA. Vogelsong blew out his arm in his second appearance with the Pirates and needed reconstructive surgery. When he was healthy enough to return, he wasn't very good. Vogelsong was pounded in an early season start at Chicago in 2004, and afterward stopped by manager Lloyd McClendon's office to say, "That will never happen again." But it did happen again, and it happened fairly often. Vogelsong wound up 10–19 with a 6.01 ERA in his 103 games with the Pirates. Rios wrecked his knee in his second game with the Pirates and stuck around for one mediocre season before he was released.

The Pirates had been on an interesting streak with pitchers who were about to become too expensive. On March 17, 1992, they traded 20-game winner John Smiley to Minnesota and got left-hander Denny Neagle. After Neagle became a consistent winner, the Pirates traded him to Atlanta on August 28, 1996, for Schmidt. The streak came to an abrupt halt when they dealt Schmidt for Vogelsong, a terrible trade that doomed the franchise to several more losing seasons.

DO AL OLIVER AND DAVE PARKER DESERVE TO BE IN THE HALL OF FAME?

43 Oliver and Parker were two major stars of the 1970s for the Pirates, batting champions and key members of World-Series-winning teams. Yet Oliver and Parker have struck out with Hall of Fame voters. Oliver's first entry on the ballot got him just 19 votes, which knocked him out of future consideration. Parker has gotten enough support to stay eligible for election, but he's never come close to the 75 percent approval rate needed for election.

Both players were signed and developed by the Pirates. Oliver came up as a first baseman, but played most of his career in center field. The Pirates traded him to Texas in

1977, and Oliver wound up playing for seven teams, including six in his last five seasons. Oliver was a feared hitter who had a penchant for making solid contact. He never had a home run stroke, managing just 219 homers in his 18 seasons. Oliver won one batting championship, posting a .331 average with Montreal in 1982. He also led the league that season with 109 RBIs, one of two times in his career that he topped 100. Oliver ranked among the top ten in RBIs just four times in his career and never scored 100 runs. He finished with a .303 average, and 1,326 RBIs. His postseason play was undistinguished: In seven series, covering 92 at-bats, he hit .228 with 3 home runs and 17 RBIs.

Oliver finished 257 hits short of 3,000, and can probably blame that on being in the wrong place at the wrong time. Near the end of his career, he was with National League teams (Giants, Dodgers, Phillies) when he was best suited for designated hitter duties. Oliver was never more than an average defensive player, and his skills eroded later in his career. He was such a defensive liability that in 1984, the Phillies offered a bonus to any of their scouts who could find a deal that would move Oliver's contract. Had he spent a couple of those seasons in the American League, his chances of reaching 3,000 hits would have been enhanced, and his consideration for the Hall would have increased, too.

Parker looked like he was a shoo-in for the Hall in the

early part of his career. He was a dominating player who combined batting average, power, speed, and a much-feared throwing arm. Parker led the National League in hitting in 1977 and 1978 and was the league's Most Valuable Player in 1978 as well. That production earned him one of the game's biggest contracts, a five-year deal that paid close to $1 million per year, with incentives.

That contract proved to be Parker's downfall. He became complacent and admitted he started using drugs. He neglected conditioning and gained weight, checking in at nearly 300 pounds. His game suffered, and the added weight led to injury problems. In his last four years with the Pirates, he hit just 44 home runs, and his batting average sunk as low as .258. The Pirates were paying superstar money for an average player, and had no interest in retaining Parker when his contract was up. He found similar apathy on the free agent market. His only significant offer came from his hometown Cincinnati Reds.

That slight motivated Parker to get in shape. He resurrected his career with the Reds, although he was never as good as he had been with the Pirates. He played for five teams and wound up with a .290 average, 339 home runs, and 1,493 RBIs in 19 seasons. He was a designated hitter for 484 games. Parker's statistics compare to those of Tony Perez, who is in the Hall of Fame. But Perez is considered a marginal choice by many, a player whose statistics don't support his hearsay reputation as a great clutch player.

Did Parker's drug use cost him a shot at the Hall? It probably did, but not as a character issue. Parker didn't take care of himself, and his game suffered in what should have been peak years. His worst years with the Pirates came from ages 29 to 32, when he should have been at his best. The ordinary numbers he put up then dragged down his career totals and diminished the amount of support he gets in the balloting. He fell 288 hits short of 3,000.

Our verdict? Well, Oliver fell short of 3,000 hits, never had much power, and was not a strong defensive player. Parker can look back on his career with regret, because it took a downward spiral in his middle years that was self-inflicted. Neither ex-Pirate has a strong case for a place in the Hall.

DID DOCK ELLIS REALLY PITCH A NO-HITTER UNDER THE INFLUENCE OF LSD?

 44 Dock Ellis was a diva before anyone was using that term to describe those addicted to the spotlight. He was also a pretty good pitcher for the Pirates for eight years, going 96–80 from

1968 to 1975. But Ellis loved attention, so he's better remembered for flaps on and off the field than he is for his pitching. His best-known controversy came years after his career ended: He claimed he pitched a 1970 no-hitter under the influence of LSD.

To put it in context, this certainly wasn't the only oddity regarding Ellis. There was the game in 1974 when he decided to send a message to the Cincinnati Reds and tried to hit every batter. Another time Ellis got into a hassle with a security guard at Cincinnati's Riverfront Stadium and was sprayed with mace as he tried to enter the park. And you can't forget the day at Wrigley Field when a wire service photographer spotted Ellis wearing hair curlers in pregame drills and sent the picture nationwide. When the Pirates made it to the postseason in 1971, Ellis made headlines by complaining his hotel bed was too small.

Ellis's favorite phrase was "wolf tickets—somebody's always selling them, somebody's always buying them." Wolf tickets were stories that may or may not have been true. Ellis delighted in keeping the line between fact and fiction blurry. He was from Los Angeles and reporters often assumed he was a street kid from a tough neighborhood. He did nothing to discourage that perception. The fact was Ellis was raised in a working-class neighborhood in a stable and caring two-parent household, but the stories alleging that he was from Watts made things more interesting.

Ellis had a good career, but was probably never as consistently successful as he should have been. He later admitted that alcohol and drugs had been a distraction throughout his time in baseball, which brings us back to the alleged LSD-fueled game.

Ellis dropped the bombshell in 1984 by telling reporters that he had been under the influence of LSD when he pitched a no-hitter against the San Diego Padres on June 12, 1970.

The Pirates had an open date between Los Angeles and San Diego. As Ellis puts it, he remained in Los Angeles to party with friends. Somehow, the off day got away from him and he didn't realize it was Friday, his day to pitch the first game of a doubleheader against the Padres. He scrambled to get to the airport and said he arrived at the ballpark at 4:30, about ninety minutes before he was scheduled to pitch. Ellis said his memories of the game were spotty, but that he remembered being in a euphoric state. He said sometimes he could see catcher Jerry May, but there were times when the catcher disappeared, too. Whatever the case, the game took just 2 hours and 13 minutes. The Padres were a light-hitting bunch whose .246 team average was third from last in the National League. Ellis baffled them, walking eight batters and hitting another while not allowing a hit.

So had he taken LSD? The pitcher seemed to be lucid in postgame interviews, and no teammates recalled seeing anything different in his behavior. The wildness would seem to support his claim, but a high walk total is not unprecedented in a dominating performance. Bill Bevens of the Yankees walked ten Brooklyn Dodgers in game 4 of the 1947 World Series and came within an out of a no-hitter. Steve Barber of the Baltimore Orioles walked ten Yankees in 8⅔ innings while not allowing a hit in 1967. Sometimes the pitches are so lively that they're as hard to control as they are to hit.

There's no reason to doubt that Ellis took LSD during his career. It was a fashionable drug at the time, and Ellis had a proclivity for sampling new things. The question is whether he took it in the timeframe he recalled, and whether he was still under the influence when he faced the Padres. Pitching is a complex exercise, and it's difficult to believe someone who's impaired could last for nine innings and decipher signals from a catcher he didn't always see. A lot of his teammates roll their eyes at the story, convinced it's just Dock grabbing the spotlight one more time.

There's no way to know for sure, so we have to take Ellis's word. Just be aware there's enough doubt to suggest the story could be his ultimate wolf ticket.

WHY DID THE PIRATES HAVE ATTENDANCE PROBLEMS IN THE 1970s?

45 General manager Joe L. Brown thought he didn't have to worry about attendance for Pirates games in the 1970s. He had a winning team and a brand new stadium. He figured all they had to do was open the gates and wait for the stampede. Maybe that was the problem.

By 1978, Pirates' attendance was 11th in the 12-team National League. Despite an exciting contending team, the Pirates failed to crack the 1 million barrier, drawing just 964,106 fans. The Pirates went down to the last weekend of the season fighting for the National League East title with the Philadelphia Phillies. Pittsburgh yawned.

What happened? Following are the top theories.

THE STADIUM WAS MORE DETRIMENTAL THAN HELPFUL

Three Rivers was a bad baseball park, and the word-of-mouth communication on that point was swift. It wasn't a good place to watch a game and access was difficult. Even modest-sized crowds of 20,000 would lead to monumental traffic jams. People stuck in the car with cranky kids were not likely to be return customers. Plus, the stadium had too many seats, so there was never an urgency to buy tickets in advance. That made the Pirates' sales more vulnerable to factors such as bad weather and losing streaks.

THE TEAM WON TOO MUCH

Strange as it sounds, even winning can get boring. That's especially the case when the winning falls short of a championship. The Pirates won their division in five out of six years from 1970 to 1975, but advanced to the World Series just once. Fans got into the habit of a successful regular season, followed by postseason disappointment. The mind-set is not unique to Pittsburgh. In recent years the Atlanta Braves have had their regular-season success work against them. Fans are blasé about winning, and don't take the Braves seriously unless they get to the World Series. Winning the division over a 162-game schedule is a major test for a team, but it got old for Pittsburgh fans when the Pirates consistently failed to go any further.

THE STEELERS WERE TAKING OVER

The Pirates' winning their division paled in comparison to the Super Bowl trophies the Steelers brought home four times. Besides, it was more fun to identify with a team that boasted Jack Lambert and Joe Greene and that physically intimidated opponents. Slipping a slider past a good hitter didn't bring the same measure of satisfaction that laying out a quarterback did. The Steelers made Pittsburgh proud, and the Pirates got lost in the shuffle.

THE PIRATES TOOK THE FANS FOR GRANTED

Because Brown was an old-school type who believed baseball was the most important product, the Pirates only did a few promotions. Unfortunately for him, this came in an era when other teams—such as the Philadelphia Phillies—were aggressively marketing with special events and giveaways. When the Pirates tried to get up to speed, they were playing catch-up to the rest of the industry. They hired an advertising agency, which created the memorable "Lumber Company" identity, but there was much ground to be made up. The Pirates set themselves back further by alienating fans with the decision to endorse KDKA radio's firing of popular announcers Bob Prince and Nellie King in 1975.

THE PIRATES WEREN'T THAT APPEALING

The team always seemed to have players who weren't easy to like. Nobody had warm and fuzzy feelings about Pirates such as John Candelaria and Dave Parker, while the Steelers offered fans far more palatable figures. Indeed,

Steelers Franco Harris and Joe Greene were in demand for commercials because of their popularity.

So which is the real reason for the Pirates' attendance problem? All of them. They all added up to disappointing business at the box office. In 1971 and 1972, the first two full seasons at Three Rivers, the Pirates ranked fifth in attendance in the National League. In their World Series year of 1979, they were tenth, with attendance of 1.4 million. It was one of the most successful stretches in franchise history, yet the team just couldn't overcome its troubles to lure in the fans.

WHAT WERE THE PIRATES' WORST SIGNINGS?

46 Incredibly, the Pirates, who poormouth their way through baseball's choppy economic waters, spent $108 million in 1999 and 2000. You'd never know it from their on-the-field performance.

It took just over two years to write the checks, but many more were spent regretting them. There were four signings:

KEVIN YOUNG, $24 MILLION FOR FOUR YEARS

Young had perfect timing, putting up big numbers in 1999 (.298 average, 26 home runs, and 106 runs batted in) just when he was due for a new contract. The Pirates, sensitive to the perception that they always let players get away, signed him for four years. Over the remainder of the contract, he batted .243 and averaged thirteen home runs and 53 RBIs per season. The Pirates wound up releasing him before the contract ended. Even though he played well in 1999, the Pirates should have been wary. Young had been released by both the Pirates and the Kansas City Royals earlier in his career, and he had chronically bad knees, which wound up being a major factor in his decline.

PAT MEARES, $15 MILLION FOR FOUR YEARS

Meares's signing was positively baffling. The Pirates picked him up for the 1999 season after the Minnesota Twins had declined to offer him a contract (that should have been a clue). Even then, he didn't look like a bad investment as a one-year stopgap for $1.5 million. Inexplicably, general manager Cam Bonifay then rushed to lock him up long term, even though he was 30 years old and the kind of player who could be easily replaced. Over the life of that contract, Meares wound up with just 823 at-bats, hitting .238 with 17 home runs, 79 RBIs, and 36 errors.

116

A hand injury essentially ruined his career, but he wasn't a star before the injury and subsequent surgery, either. The Pirates wound up reclaiming some of the money on an insurance claim.

JASON KENDALL, $60 MILLION FOR SEVEN YEARS

Kendall wasn't a bad player. He just wasn't worth the money the Pirates lavished on him. Kendall was a singles-hitting catcher who wound up being paid a cleanup hitter's salary. He wasn't an impact player, but that didn't stop the Pirates from misjudging his value and giving him the richest contract in club history. Even more amazing, it came a year after his 1999 gruesome ankle dislocation, a major injury that raised questions about his long-term future. The Pirates thought Kendall could be the face of the franchise, ignoring his aversion to making public appearances and the open contempt he had for a lot of teammates. The Pirates wound up giving Kendall to the Oakland Athletics in 2005 just to get some financial relief. They were still on the hook for part of his 2007 salary, though, so the effects of this contract lingered.

DEREK BELL, $9 MILLION FOR TWO YEARS

Bell is one of baseball's most celebrated free agent mistakes. The Pirates thought they were getting a legitimate middle-of-the-order hitter. His signing led manager

Lloyd McClendon to proclaim that the Pirates were sending "shock waves" through baseball. Bonifay said, "He's in the prime of his career." The Pirates apparently hadn't noticed that Bell had hit just .187 in the second half of the 2000 season and that the New York Mets had no interest in bringing him back. Bell appeared in only 46 games for the Pirates, batting .173 with 5 home runs and 13 RBIs. He spent a good part of 2001 on the disabled list, and the Pirates were in no rush to activate him because they knew he couldn't help. Bell was released the next year in spring training. He was surprised to learn that he had to compete for a job and told a reporter he planned to go into "Operation Shutdown" as a response. He'd actually done that the year before—and his signing was one of the last straws that cost Bonifay his job in June of 2001. Bell's signing was so wrong on so many levels that it came to symbolize the futility of the Pirates in the new century.

The tab on bad contracts was almost more than $108 million. Bonifay offered mediocre third baseman Ed Sprague a multi-year deal in 1999, but Sprague foolishly turned it down. It was one instance where a player's judgement was worse than the team's.

PENGUINS POINTS

WHO WAS THE PENGUINS' BEST PLAYER BEFORE MARIO LEMIEUX?

47 The fortunes of the Penguins changed forever on June 9, 1984, when they drafted Mario Lemieux. The franchise that had never won anything added one of the most talented players in the history of the NHL, found itself with a genuine drawing card, and became the focal point of the league. From the moment Lemieux's name was called at the draft, Penguins history became divided into pre-Mario and post-Mario. Although the Penguins still missed the playoffs in Lemieux's first four seasons, there was obvious improvement. The team's point total increased by 15 in Lemieux's first season, then took another 23-point leap in his second season. By Lemieux's fifth season, the Penguins were in the playoffs and had improved by 49 points since his arrival. The team won its first championship in 1991 and immediately started filling the Civic Arena as the fan base expanded beyond the hard-core fans who had supported the Penguins in the early days.

In the 17 seasons before Lemieux, the Penguins missed the playoffs eight times and were eliminated in the first round six times. The closest they came to success was the 1974–1975 season, when they beat St. Louis in the first round and took a 3–0 lead in their second-round series against the New York Islanders. But the Penguins became just the second team in NHL history to lose a series after winning the first three games. They scored only 5 goals in those last four games. Worse, the team fell into bankruptcy that summer and was in danger of folding or being moved.

Believe it or not, though, it wasn't all bad pre-Lemieux. The Penguins had some good players...just not enough of them. Here's a look at five standouts who preceded Mario.

5. RANDY CARLYLE, DEFENSEMAN, 1978–1979 TO 1983–1984

Carlyle was an offensive defenseman who proved to be an excellent quarterback for the power play. He wasn't especially strong in his own end, but his offensive production helped make up for those shortcomings. Carlyle had 16 goals and 83 points in 1980–1981 and became the only Penguin to win the Norris Trophy as the NHL's best defenseman.

4. DAVE BURROWS, DEFENSEMAN, 1971–1972 TO 1977–1978 AND 1980–1981

Burrows was the anti-Carlyle, a stay-at-home defenseman who played a solid fundamental game and took care of the defensive zone. The NHL didn't keep blocked shots as an official stat then, otherwise it would be easier to quantify Burrows's value to the Penguins. He never had more than 7 goals or 29 points in a season, but his game was goal prevention. And he was good at it.

3. SYL APPS, CENTER, 1970–1971 TO 1977–1978

Apps was a gifted scorer who gave the Penguins six full seasons of solid production. His best year was 1975–1976, when he had 32 goals and 99 points as part of the "Century Line" with Lowell MacDonald and Jean Pronovost. The second-generation NHLer was stolen from the New York Rangers in a trade that ranks as one of general manager Jack Riley's best deals.

2. PIERRE LAROUCHE, CENTER, 1974–1975 TO 1977–1978

Larouche made headlines in his three and a half years with the Penguins, sometimes for the wrong reasons. He was spectacular in 1975–1976, scoring 53 goals with 111 points. The next year he slumped to 29 goals and 63 points, which was the beginning of the end for him in

Pittsburgh. Larouche had maturity issues, which led to frequent clashes with coach Ken Schinkel and an eventual giveaway trade to Montreal early in the 1977–1978 season. Larouche, only 22 years old at the time of the trade, played 572 more NHL games with Montreal, Hartford, and the New York Rangers. He had a 50-goal season with the Canadiens in 1979–1980 and scored 48 points for the Rangers in 1983–1984.

1. JEAN PRONOVOST, RIGHT WING, 1968–1969 TO 1977–1978

Larouche was the most talented player before Lemieux, but Pronovost was the most productive. He had at least 20 goals in each of his ten seasons and scored 52 goals with 104 points in 1975–1976. He became more prolific as the NHL opened up and he had at least 40 goals in four of his last five years with the Penguins from 1973–1974 to 1977–1978. Pronovost played 753 games for the Penguins, scoring 316 goals and 603 points. His consistency is even more amazing considering the Penguins' annual training camp tests showed he had below-average peripheral vision. Pronovost learned how to anticipate the play and compensate for his weakness so that it was never noticed on the ice.

WHO WERE THE PENGUINS' BEST FIGHTERS?

There was a time when every National Hockey League team carried at least one player who made his living with his fists. If that player was on your favorite team, he was an "enforcer." If he played for a rival team, he was a "goon."

In a bygone era some of the fighters could also play hockey, too. That's how the term "Gordie Howe hat trick" developed, to designate a game in which a player had a goal, assist, and a major penalty for fighting. It was part of hockey's culture, especially when the sport was primarily Canadian. But fighting has slowly disappeared from the NHL because of rule changes and a general evolution: more NHL players come from Europe and colleges, and aren't steeped in tradition of dropping the gloves to slug it out.

Still, the Penguins have a storied history of fighters. The team had Dave "The Hammer" Schultz for 113 games from 1977 to 1979, but he doesn't make our top-five list. By the time Schultz arrived in Pittsburgh, his biggest fighting days were behind him. He was accustomed to being with the Flyers, where he knew the team would follow his lead.

When he looked over his shoulder in Pittsburgh, he saw a bunch of guys sitting on the bench yelling, "Go get 'em, Schultzie." Hulking defenseman Barry Beck first came into the NHL with the Colorado Rockies in 1977, and he chased Schultz all over the ice, trying to goad him into a fight. Schultz wouldn't respond, and his reputation was damaged when he failed to answer that challenge.

Here's a look at the best heavyweights who have worn the Penguins crest over the years.

5. RICK TOCCHET

Pound for pound, this feisty winger was as tough as they come. He'd probably get a higher ranking but he played in an era where fighting was less prevalent in the game. Tocchet was fearless and his quick hands helped cut larger opponents down to size.

4. BOB "BATTLESHIP" KELLY

This rawboned winger with a wild look in his eyes was a decent player who was always quick to get involved when things got tough.

3. STEVE DURBANO

Durbano was more fighter than player, and he was committed to his work. Durbano had a wild streak and once fought his way back onto the ice after officials had sent him to the dressing room. Durbano, who died in 2002, left a legacy of stories about his explosive temper. He once went to the penalty box after a fight and asked for permission to get his skate sharpened. Officials told him stay put. Durbano removed the skate, heaved it across the ice and yelled, "Sharpen it" to the equipment man. That earned Durbano an ejection. When the period ended, the team returned to the locker room to find Durbano gone and his other skate embedded in the ceiling.

2. PAUL BAXTER

Quiet and religious away from the rink, this defenseman was a savage fighter when provoked. He piled up a team-record 409 penalty minutes in 1980–1981.

1. MARTY McSORLEY

The Penguins signed this farm boy from western Canada as an undrafted free agent mostly because of his physical presence and work ethic. Completely unpolished as a player, he worked hard and became good enough to play a regular shift, first as a defenseman, then as a winger. The big break of his career was getting traded to Edmonton, where he became Wayne Gretzky's personal bodyguard. The unspoken rule was, mess with Gretzky, deal with McSorley. Because of that, Gretzky had plenty of room. McSorley gets our vote for the Penguins' heavyweight champion for his size, relentless approach, and willingness to answer the call when any teammate was in trouble.

WHAT WERE THE PENGUINS' FIVE BEST TRADES?

49 There was a time when NHL general managers would threaten players with a trade to the Penguins. "If you don't shape up, we'll trade you to Pittsburgh" is how it usually went. The Penguins were an unsuccessful, dysfunctional organization and Pittsburgh was hockey's Siberia.

When things got better in the 1990s, there were few players who didn't welcome the opportunity to join the Penguins. The team was loaded with stars and considered a Stanley Cup contender, winning championships in 1991 and 1992. The only reason to fear coming to Pittsburgh was the concern that a player's ice time would be limited because of all the stars on the roster. It was easy to slide quickly on the Penguins' full depth chart in the early 1990s.

Here's a look at the five best trades in franchise history.

5. SYL APPS AND SHELDON KANNEGIESSER FROM THE NEW YORK RANGERS FOR GLEN SATHER, 1971

General manager Jack Riley made this trade, which was instantly unpopular with Penguins fans. They loved Sather's feisty style, but soon forgot about that when they saw Apps's scoring touch. Sather's grit was easily replaced, while Apps became a star for the Penguins. His ninety-nine points in 1975–1976 set a club record at the time.

4. RANDY CARLYLE AND GEORGE FERGUSON FROM THE TORONTO MAPLE LEAFS FOR DAVE BURROWS, 1978

General manager Baz Bastien had perfect timing on this deal. Burrows was a rock-steady defenseman, but his career had peaked. Carlyle was the opposite of Burrows, a defenseman who liked to rush the puck. He quarterbacked a power play that would set an NHL record for goals. Carlyle won the Norris Trophy in 1981. Ferguson was a fast-skating winger with a nice scoring touch.

3. KEVIN STEVENS FROM THE LOS ANGELES KINGS FOR ANDERS HAKANSON, 1983

This didn't break out of the agate-type of transactions when general manager Eddie Johnston made the trade. Yet Stevens, a big, rowdy winger from Boston College, wound up being a key component in the Penguins' two championships. In addition to his scoring (four seasons with at least 40 goals, 1990 to 1994), Stevens was a vocal leader. He was the one who stood up and promised that the Penguins would win their 1991 playoff series against the Boston Bruins after falling behind two games to none. The Penguins won the next four games and went on to claim the Stanley Cup.

2. LARRY MURPHY AND PETER TAGLIANETTI FROM MINNESOTA FOR JIM JOHNSON AND CHRIS DAHLQUIST, DECEMBER 11, 1990

This trade involving four defensemen brought the Penguins Larry Murphy, an offensive presence on the blue line. He manned the point on the power play and helped get the puck to Mario Lemieux and the rest of the talented forwards. Murphy secured his Hall of Fame credentials while playing on Pittsburgh's two Cup-winning teams.

1. RON FRANCIS, ULF SAMUELSSON, AND GRANT JENNINGS FROM HARTFORD FOR JOHN CULLEN, ZARLEY ZALAPSKI, AND JEFF PARKER, MARCH 4, 1991

This deal worked out so perfectly for the Penguins, it's easy to forget the Whalers didn't get fleeced in the trade. Cullen was a productive forward who had 31 goals and 94 points at the time of the trade. Zalapski's speed brought comparisons to Paul Coffey. But Francis, who had inexplicably fallen into disfavor in Hartford, was the perfect number-2 center the Penguins needed behind Mario Lemieux. Samuelsson was the physical defenseman and irritant who helped the Penguins succeed through four rounds of playoffs. Eddie Johnston was Hartford's general manager when this deal was made. When Johnston was fired after the 1992 season, Pittsburgh general manager Craig Patrick immediately found a spot for him in the Penguins organization. It was the least Patrick could have done for a man who'd had a hand in the most important trade in Penguins history.

WHAT WERE THE PENGUINS' FIVE WORST TRADES?

50 For the longest time, financial concerns overruled foresight for the Penguins.

Their mission was just to make the playoffs and squeeze some extra revenue out of a few postseason games. Until owner Edward DeBartolo Sr. authorized a full building program in 1983, there was never a long-term vision. Taking it one season at a time led to some bad trades.

It's interesting, though, that three of the five on this list were made by Craig Patrick, who was—by far—the most astute general manager the Penguins ever had. Of course, he was on the job for 17 years, longer than anyone, so it stands to reason that he'd have some clunkers among the deals that helped win a pair of Stanley Cups.

Here's a look at five trades the Penguins wound up regretting.

5. JAROMIR JAGR TO THE WASHINGTON CAPITALS FOR KRIS BEECH, ROSS LUPASCHUCK, AND MICHAEL SIVEK, 2001

Patrick's hands were tied to some degree on this one. He had1 to move Jagr because the Penguins could no longer afford him, and his sullen attitude was poisoning the dressing room. Jagr famously declared himself "dying alive" in Pittsburgh and said he needed to get out. Only two teams could handle Jagr's whopping contract, and Patrick picked the wrong one. He dealt his troubled star for three players who would score a total of 10 goals for the Penguins, or the output Jagr could often provide in a month.

Ordinarily trades forced by finances get a pass, but this is a case where Patrick apparently rejected a better offer from the New York Rangers because of a personal conflict with Rangers general manager Glen Sather. Larry Brooks has reported in the *New York Post* that the Rangers were willing to give up Mike York and Kim Johnsson in a trade for Jagr. That would have been significantly better than the package of nothing that came from Washington.

4. FIRST-ROUND DRAFT PICK IN 1979 TO WASHINGTON FOR HARTLAND MONAHAN, 1977

Beleaguered general manager Baz Bastien always took the heat for this one, but it wasn't his deal. The Penguins played Washington in the second game of the 1977–1978 season and owner Al Savill was impressed with Monahan. He got on the phone to the Capitals and agreed to give up his future number-one draft pick for a forward the Penguins didn't especially need. That became clear a month later when Bastien packaged Monahan in a deal with the Los Angeles Kings. Monahan played seven games for the Penguins and scored 2 goals. The Penguins' drafting position wound up being tenth in 1979 and among the players available at that point were forwards Michel Goulet, Duane Sutter, and Brian Propp, along with defensemen Kevin Lowe and Mike Ramsey.

Trivia note: Monahan married the daughter of hockey Hall of Famer Bernie "Boom Boom" Geoffrion, and their son, Shane Monahan, played baseball for the Seattle Mariners.

3. GLEN MURRAY TO THE LOS ANGELES KINGS FOR EDDIE OLCZYK, 1991

This was a deadline-day deal designed to fill a need for a checking forward and penalty killer down the stretch. There was nothing wrong with that idea, but the Penguins paid too steep a price by giving up Murray, a hard-working forward with a scoring touch.

After leaving Pittsburgh, Murray had two seasons with 29 goals and three others with at least 30. The slow-skating Olczyk played a part-time role for the Penguins for a couple of seasons, then returned after retirement to work as a color analyst on television before he was hired as head coach. Selecting the inexperienced Olczyk as head coach was a bad move, but not as bad as giving up Murray for a role player.

2. MARKUS NASLUND TO VANCOUVER FOR ALEX STOJANOV, 1997

This was another deadline deal gone awry. In fairness to the Penguins, the timid Naslund had chances to play but could never crack the top two lines. He often seemed to be intimidated by the team's talent level. So again the Penguins at least had a reasonable idea—trade some of their offensive surplus for muscle that could help in the playoffs.

Stojanov was 6 feet 4 inches and 232 pounds, and had once piled up 270 penalty minutes in a minor league season. He played just 45 games over two seasons for the

133

Penguins and contributed very little. Stojanov was seriously injured in a car accident during his time with the Penguins, but that didn't prevent him from playing five minor league seasons after he left Pittsburgh. Naslund, meanwhile, blossomed into a first-rate forward and gained confidence in his game. He has had six seasons with at least 30 goals for Vancouver.

1. GEORGE FERGUSON AND THE NUMBER-ONE DRAFT CHOICE TO MINNESOTA FOR ANDERS HAKANSSON, RON MEIGHAN, AND MINNESOTA'S NUMBER-ONE DRAFT CHOICE

There's plenty of blame to go around for this one. Coach Eddie Johnston had soured on Ferguson and told general manager Baz Bastien to trade him. Bastien made a seemingly innocuous early-season deal, trading Ferguson to Minnesota for Hakansson, a so-so forward, and Meighan, a lanky defenseman who had been Minnesota's number-one draft choice in 1981. But the other component—a swap of first-round drafting positions—is what makes this the worst of the worst.

At the time, the Penguins were thinking they and the North Stars would be somewhere around the middle of the NHL pack. They figured they'd be moving down just a few spots in the draft order. However, the Penguins sunk in the standings and finished dead last, which gave them the number-one overall pick. Instead of having control of the entire draft, the Penguins had to wait until the 15th spot to take Minnesota's place. They watched other teams take Steve Yzerman, Cam Neely, Pat LaFontaine, and John MacLean, while they settled for checking line forward Bob Errey at the 15th selection.

But the sting of that mistake taught a valuable lesson. When the Penguins were headed for another last-place finish in the 1983–1984 season, they held onto the top pick. They used it to select Mario Lemieux and forever changed the franchise.

WHAT WAS THE PENGUINS' BIGGEST DRAFT BLUNDER?

51 Anyone who wonders why the Penguins couldn't sustain any success before Mario Lemieux arrived in 1984 need only look at the team's draft record. When they weren't trading away their top pick for some short-term help, the Penguins were picking the wrong players.

Here's a look at five choices they wound up regretting.

5. RICH SUTTER, CHOSEN 10th OVERALL IN 1982

Six Sutter brothers reached the NHL, and Rich was the only one who wasn't driven to succeed. Well, at least he wasn't when the Penguins had him. He was a huge disappointment who lasted just four games into a second season, when coach Ed Johnston's patience ran out. Sutter was then shipped to Philadelphia for three average players. The jolt of the trade and the reunion with twin brother Ron helped Rich Sutter get on the right track, but he was a bust in Pittsburgh.

They could have picked: forward Dave Andreychuk, chosen 16th overall by Buffalo. He played 1,639 games with 640 goals and 1,338 points. The Penguins also could have chosen Ken Daneyko, a steady stay-at-home defenseman who was an important player on New Jersey's Stanley Cup teams. Daneyko was chosen 18th overall by the Devils.

4. PAUL MARSHALL, CHOSEN 31st OVERALL, 1979

Marshall played 49 games with the Penguins over three seasons, collecting 12 goals and 24 points. Marshall was another player who only seemed to be sporadically motivated, precisely the type Johnston didn't want. Marshall's biggest value to the Penguins came when he and Kim Davis were traded to Toronto for Paul Gardner and Dave

Burrows on November 18, 1980.

They could have picked: Mats Naslund, whom Montreal made the 37th player selected in that draft. Naslund played in 651 NHL games and scored 251 goals and 634 points. The Penguins were very late to European scouting and Naslund may not have been in their sights. Had they stayed in Canada, they could have drafted Dale Hunter, who was taken 41st overall by Quebec. Hunter played in 1,407 games with 323 goals and 1,020 points.

3. RICK KESSELL, CHOSEN 15th OVERALL, 1969

Kessell played in 134 NHL games and had four goals and 28 points. Calling him a disappointment is too mild.

They could have picked: Bob Clarke, whom the Philadelphia Flyers selected two turns later as the 17th overall pick. Clarke's Hall of Fame career included 1,144 games, 358 goals, 1,210 points, three Hart Trophies as the NHL's Most Valuable Player, and one Selke Trophy as the best defensive forward. Clarke was the heart of the Flyers teams that won two Stanley Cups and were regular contenders. Some teams were wary of drafting him because he was a diabetic, but that condition never hampered his career. If the Penguins had been scared away by Clarke's medical profile, they could have chosen Butch Goring, who was the 51st player selected. Los Angeles drafted Goring, who played 1,107 games with 375 goals and 888 points.

137

2. BRIAN McKENZIE, CHOSEN 18th OVERALL, 1971

McKenzie is obscure to even the most hardcore Penguins fan. He appeared in just six games for the Penguins with one goal and 2 points. He went on to play eighty-seven games in the World Hockey Association.

They could have picked: Craig Ramsay, who was taken by Buffalo immediately after the Penguins drafted McKenzie. Ramsay was a superior defensive forward who still managed 252 goals and 672 points in his 1,070 NHL games. He played in 776 consecutive games in one stretch. Had the Penguins been interested in a defenseman, future Hall of Famer Larry Robinson lasted until Montreal made him the 20th player selected. Robinson won two Norris Trophies as the NHL's best defenseman and was the Most Valuable Player of the 1978 playoffs.

1. GORD LAXTON, CHOSEN 13th OVERALL, 1975

The Penguins went shopping for a goalie and came away with Laxton, who had posted good but not great statistics with the New Westminster Bruins in junior hockey: wrong choice. Laxton appeared in 17 NHL games over four seasons, posting a 4–9 record and a goals-against average of 5.92.

The shame of this choice (and the reason it's number one) is that there were two much better goaltenders available and the Buffalo Sabres got both of them. Bob Sauve was drafted 17th overall and won 182 games over 13 seasons. His goals-against average was 3.48. His partner was Don Edwards, who was the 89th player chosen in the draft. Edwards won 208 games and had a 3.32 goals-against average. He and Sauve shared the Vezina Trophy in 1979–1980. Gord Laxton went to the minor leagues that season and never returned to the NHL.

WHO REALLY SAVED HOCKEY IN PITTSBURGH?

There's no question Mario Lemieux's presence made the Penguins successful for the first time and created interest that pushed the sport from its cult status closer to mainstream popularity.

In the 17 seasons before Lemieux arrived in 1984, the Penguins had 44 sellouts, an average of less than three per season. In 1988–1989 and again in 1989–1990, they had 34 sellouts in each season. This happened despite the fact that the seating capacity of the Civic Arena grew by about 3,000 from the early days of the franchise, and the price of tickets rose steadily as well.

The Penguins averaged 6,839 in attendance in 1983–1984, the last season before Lemieux arrived. That figure rose to 10,018 the next season and was over 15,000 by 1987–1988. You don't need a calculator to see that Lemieux's presence had a huge effect in ticket revenue, still the main source of income for NHL teams.

But suggesting that the Penguins wouldn't have survived in Pittsburgh without Lemieux requires a leap of logic that can't be definitively made. The Penguins and New Jersey Devils went down the stretch in the 1983–1984 season in a battle to see who would post the worst record and "win" the right to select Lemieux with the first overall pick in the draft. (This was before the NHL instituted a draft lottery for the nonplayoff teams.) The Penguins finished last, with 38 points, and thus got to select Lemieux. The Devils had 41 points and settled for Kirk Muller in the second drafting spot.

Muller was a fine player who helped the Devils. He was not Mario Lemieux.

Yet, despite losing in the Lemieux derby in 1984, let's look at what's happened to the franchises since that season. The Devils have won three Stanley Cup championships and advanced to the finals one other time. The Penguins won two Cups. Since 1983–1984, the Devils have finished out of the playoffs five times. The Penguins have had nine seasons in which they didn't qualify for the postseason. The Penguins also went bankrupt in November of

1998 and crawled out of that mess by sacrificing star players with big contracts in order to gain financial relief.

So while Lemieux's importance to the Penguins can't be understated, it is inaccurate to say the franchise wouldn't have survived without him. The Devils didn't get him and they not only survived, they've had more success than the Penguins have enjoyed in the same timeframe.

The person who really saved hockey for Pittsburgh probably never put on a pair of skates in his life. Edward DeBartolo Sr. was a slightly built man with a serious mien who made his fortune building shopping malls. He originally got involved with the Penguins in 1977, purchasing a one-third share to bail out an ownership group that was running short of money. A year later DeBartolo was in control. People who worked for the Penguins noticed. Suddenly the smallest purchases required authorization from DeBartolo headquarters in Youngstown, Ohio. Complimentary tickets, once abundant, were shut off. The Penguins were being run like a business.

Despite the emphasis on fiscal responsibility, DeBartolo was willing to absorb losses to give the Penguins a legitimate chance to win. General manager Eddie Johnston outlined a 1983 blueprint in which the Penguins would be stripped down and started from scratch. DeBartolo approved it. Veterans were jettisoned for prospects and draft choices. The Penguins focused on the long range for the first time, rather than just trying to squeeze into the playoff field to collect the extra revenue from a few home games.

As the Penguins improved, DeBartolo signed off on expensive acquisitions such as Paul Coffey and Tom Barrasso. Eventually, the Penguins built a winner. DeBartolo, who once called hockey a lousy investment, celebrated by selling the franchise.

At the first Stanley Cup celebration in 1991, some people booed when DeBartolo was introduced. They perceived him as a stern man who had no real affection for the sport. But he deserved a standing ovation, because Edward DeBartolo Sr. saved hockey for Pittsburgh.

WHAT WERE CRAIG PATRICK'S BEST MOVES AS PENGUINS GENERAL MANAGER?

53 The Penguins made one of the most important decisions in their history when they hired Craig Patrick as general manager on December 5, 1989.

Patrick replaced Tony Esposito as general manager, and also took over as coach, replacing Gene Ubriaco. Patrick was never more than an average coach, but working the bench for the last 54 games of the 1989–1990 season allowed him to see the team up close every day and get a feel for the locker room chemistry as well.

Patrick came to Pittsburgh with an impressive history. Born to a hockey family (the Patrick Division the Penguins played in was named for his grandfather, Lester Patrick), he was also Herb Brooks's assistant coach on the 1980 "Miracle on Ice" Olympic team. He helped the University of Denver win two NCAA championships as a player in the 1960s, and became the youngest general manager in the history of the New York Rangers at age 35 in 1981.

Patrick moved aggressively and put his imprint on an organization that had talented players but didn't know how to win. His specialty was adding to the impressive base of talent. Patrick was able to spot the specific needs the Penguins had, then make deals to acquire the talent the organization was lacking. In less than two years after he signed on with the Penguins, the franchise won its first Stanley Cup.

Here's a look at the five moves Patrick made that transformed the Penguins.

5. ACQUIRED LEFT WING JOE MULLEN FROM CALGARY FOR A SECOND-ROUND DRAFT CHOICE ON JUNE 16, 1990

This deal proved that it's not always a mistake to trade a prime draft choice for an older player. Mullen was 33 when the deal was made, but he was the kind of smart, experienced player who was a tremendous asset through the Stanley Cup championship runs in 1991 and 1992. Mullen had 17 points in 22 games during the playoffs in the first Cup year. He scored 42 goals the following season.

4. ACQUIRED DEFENSEMEN LARRY MURPHY AND PETER TAGLIANETTI FROM MINNESOTA FOR DEFENSEMEN JIM JOHNSON AND CHRIS DAHLQUIST ON DECEMBER 11, 1990

Patrick gave up two ordinary players and got Murphy, a future Hall of Famer who was an integral part of the Cup teams.

3. DRAFTED JAROMIR JAGR IN THE FIRST ROUND (FOURTH OVERALL) IN 1990

While it may have been impossible to overlook Jagr's talent and potential, Patrick was the one general manager with the nerve to take him in the first round. Getting players out of the Czech Republic was still a complicated process. Patrick did his homework and was confident he had the means to bring Jagr to North America. He was correct, and the Penguins had a franchise-caliber talent to add to an already impressive collection of scorers.

2. HIRED BOB JOHNSON AS COACH AND SCOTTY BOWMAN AS DIRECTOR OF PLAYER DEVELOPMENT AND RECRUITMENT ON JUNE 12, 1990

Patrick didn't just hire a coach and personnel advisor, he created a virtual hockey think-tank by recruiting two of the sharpest minds in the game. The always-optimistic Johnson was a perfect choice for a team that had grown jaded to

145

authority after running off coaches Pierre Creamer and Gene Ubriaco. And with Bowman, Patrick managed to bring in his wisdom but put him in a role where his abrasive personality wouldn't be a factor. Bowman basically consulted with Patrick and Bob Johnson, and both were secure enough to handle Bowman's legendary bluntness. Both Johnson and Bowman came from outside the organization with no preconceived notions about the Penguins or their talent. The fresh approach was a big factor in turning around the franchise.

1. ACQUIRED CENTER RON FRANCIS, DEFENSEMAN ULF SAMUELSSON, AND DEFENSEMAN GRANT JENNINGS FROM HARTFORD FOR CENTER JOHN CULLEN, DEFENSEMAN ZARLEY ZALAPSKI, AND FORWARD JEFF PARKER ON MARCH 4, 1991

Patrick knew he had enough goal scorers and could deal Cullen. He knew he was two-deep in offensive defensemen with Paul Coffey and Larry Murphy, which allowed him to trade Zalapski. He got the number-2 center he needed in Francis, along with Samuelsson, the physical defenseman the Penguins were lacking. Patrick also jolted the psyche of a team that hadn't yet secured a playoff spot. The deal has become the standard by which all other deadline deals are judged, which says something about the impact this move had. It capped a phenomenally successful start for Patrick, who was drinking from the Stanley Cup after his first full season with the Penguins.

WHAT WERE THE SIGNS IT WAS TIME FOR CRAIG PATRICK TO LEAVE?

Without question, Patrick was the most successful general manager the Penguins have ever had.

He came in as an outsider, refusing to accept the idea that the franchise was destined to fail. He changed the mind-set and helped turn the Penguins into one of the NHL's elite organizations. It helped that he worked for owners who had open checkbooks. Edward DeBartolo Sr. had enough money to support a big payroll, and subsequent owner Howard Baldwin was able to temporarily fool people into thinking he did, too. But Baldwin's house of cards eventually collapsed and the Penguins were in bankruptcy court for the second time in franchise history in 1998.

Limited funds made a huge difference in the way the

Penguins did business. But Patrick also changed. He showed loyalty to long-term employees who were no longer effective. The man who hired Bob Johnson and Scotty Bowman as his right-hand men was now relying on people who owed their jobs to a cronyism that weakened the Penguins. For example, Patrick employed his brother Glenn as a minor league coach despite persistent complaints from players who said they weren't being prepared properly for the NHL. By the end of Patrick's reign, the Penguins were one of the worst teams in the NHL, and there was little doubt his contract would not be renewed after the 2005–2006 season.

Here's a look at pivotal moves that turned the Penguins from a respected franchise into a dismal loser.

5. THE EUROPEAN DRAFT FIXATION

Patrick's predecessor, Tony Esposito, had an irrational dislike for European players. Patrick was open-minded and wanted talent, but seemed to go too far in the other direction, favoring European players. He hit it big with Jaromir Jagr in 1991, and Markus Naslund and Martin Straka became good players, too. But the Penguins reached too many times and came up with disappointments such as Aleksey Morozov, Konstantin Koltsov, and Milan Kraft, and absolute flops such as Robert Dome.

4. FAILURE TO ESTABLISH A SENSE OF AUTHORITY

The Penguins had superstars, and players like that often have egos. That's how the Penguins got a reputation for being coach killers. Patrick addressed that in 1991 when he hired Bob Johnson, an experienced coach who could establish order without stifling the players. After Johnson's death in November of 1991, Scotty Bowman took over and the players chafed. Patrick eased up, choosing Ed Johnston to follow Bowman. Johnston couldn't maintain the level of success, so Patrick took one last shot at clamping down by hiring Kevin Constantine. But when the players rebelled, Constantine was gone, and Patrick went back to coaches who were going to be acceptable to the players.

3. BAD TRADES

The Penguins' financial plight limited what Patrick could do. He couldn't keep stars who had big contracts, and every NHL team knew he was dealing from a position of weakness. For example, Patrick had to get rid of Jaromir Jagr, and decided to ship him to Washington. But the New York Rangers insist they made a better offer than Washington did for Jagr. The Rangers maintain that Patrick dealt Jagr to Washington because he was angry with Rangers general manager Glen Sather. Spite is no way to run a business, and Patrick got the worst of the trade: instead of at least salvaging a couple of useful players in

Kim Johnsson and Mike York for the talented Jagr, the Penguins got three flops—center Kris Beech and defensemen Ross Lupaschuk and Michael Sivek. Patrick made similarly bad deals when he traded Martin Straka and Alexei Kovalev. Instead of restocking with good young players and/or draft picks, Patrick settled for players fresh off the waiver wire.

2. MISREADING THE FREE AGENT MARKET

When the NHL emerged from its 2004–2005 season-long lockout, the game had changed. Free agency was instituted, and the NHL emphasized new enforcement of rules against obstruction. The NHL was about to become a league where speed on the ice was at a premium. Patrick didn't see that, and spent some of his free agent budget on John LeClair, an old and slow winger, and tough guys such as Andre Roy and Lyle Odelein, who served no purpose in the new NHL. He also invested heavily in back-up goalie Jocelyn Thibault, who wound up taking valuable playing time away from Marc-Andre Fleury, who was the Penguins' goaltender of the future.

1. HIRING EDDIE OLCZYK AS COACH

The problem went beyond Olczyk's lack of qualifications for the job. The process was just as bad. The Penguins needed a coach for the 2003–2004 season, and Olczyk, who had been the Penguins' TV analyst, was interested.

Patrick hired him without even interviewing another candidate. Herb Brooks was interested in the job, but the Penguins didn't call him. Olczyk had no coaching experience. The Penguins knew they were short on talent that season, so coaching probably wasn't going to make a big difference. In the first season after the lockout, though, the Penguins signed free agents and had expectations of making the playoffs. Olczyk was still unproven, and he didn't even have the benefit of an experienced assistant who could help. Olczyk wound up being fired in mid-December of his second season and was replaced by Michel Therrien. But even that was somewhat of a mistake—the move should have been made in the off-season, so Therrien would have had a head start on establishing his systems. Patrick's inflexibility on this issue was the ultimate symbol that his once-magic touch was gone.

Patrick took the Penguins from a nonplayoff team to a Stanley Cup champion. Before he was finished, that journey became a depressing round trip.

WHAT WERE MARIO LEMIEUX'S FIVE GREATEST MOMENTS?

Mario Lemieux played 1,022 games for the Penguins (regular season and playoffs) in two stints from 1984 through 2006. Holding a ticket to a Penguins game then meant there was a chance to see Lemieux do something spectacular. He won 17 major NHL awards over his career, led the Penguins to a pair of Stanley Cup championships, and had a penchant for the dramatic that set him apart from other talented players.

Here's a look at the top five moments that stand out.

5. FIVE GOALS, FIVE WAYS

Lemieux found a unique way to close out 1988 in a New Year's Eve home game against New Jersey. He scored 5 goals and each one was accomplished in a different way. He became the first player to score every way possible in one game: even-strength, power play, shorthanded, penalty shot, and empty net. The Penguins beat the Devils, 8–6. (In those days, the Penguins weren't playing enough defense to assure that 5 goals were enough to win.)

4. THE DEBUT

After all the hype, all eyes were on the lanky teenager wearing No. 66 when the Penguins opened the 1984–1985 season on October 11 in Boston. Lemieux did not disappoint. On his first shift, he broke in alone on goalie Pete Peeters and beat him—first shift, first shot, first of 690 regular season goals.

3. SPLITTING STARS

In the first Stanley Cup run, Lemieux made a spectacular play in game 2 of the finals against Minnesota. He split defensemen Neil Wilkinson and Shawn Chambers—both of whom had excellent position on him—by faking to the outside to lose Chambers, then speeding past the helpless Wilkinson. Lemieux then spun and beat goalie Jon Casey with a backhander.

2. THE COMEBACK

Pittsburgh hockey fans celebrated Christmas two days late in 2000. Lemieux had announced earlier in December that he was coming back after three and a half years of retirement. Did he still have it? He did. He had a goal and two assists in the December 27 5–0 win over Toronto, and the atmosphere in Mellon Arena was as charged as it had been for Stanley Cup playoff games. The Maple Leafs were so disoriented by the experience that they never touched Lemieux, treating him as a museum piece.

1. THE OTHER COMEBACK

Lemieux took his final radiation treatment for non-Hodgkin's lymphoma disease the morning of March 2, 1993. He jumped on a private plane that afternoon and joined his teammates in Philadelphia for a game against the Flyers. He had missed 23 games while being treated for cancer. Lemieux had a goal and assist in the 5–4 loss to the Flyers, a performance that even won the approval of hardened Philadelphia fans. The loss didn't detract from the magnitude of the accomplishment. Lemieux would eventually take a season off to recover from the effects of the treatment, but that night it seemed as though he should have been wearing Superman's cape. The emotion of the night transcended hockey and made this moment the most memorable.

WHAT OTHER NUMBERS SHOULD THE PENGUINS RETIRE?

In their 40 history, the Penguins have been judicious about retiring numbers. They've taken just two out of circulation —Michel Briere's No. 21 and the No. 66 that Mario

Lemieux wore. Unlike other teams that get caught up in short-term sentiment, the Penguins have applied some thought and judgment to the process.

Their two choices are obvious. Briere had a brilliant rookie season in 1969–1970 and looked like he would become the first big star of the fledgling franchise. Shortly after that season ended, Briere was critically injured in an automobile accident and lingered in a coma for nearly a year. He died on April 13, 1971.

Lemieux set every important offensive record in team history and was immediately voted into the Hall of Fame. The only question about retiring his number was when the ceremony would be held. Besides, what player would want the burden of trying to wear No. 66 on the back of a Penguins jersey?

There are certainly other candidates to join Nos. 21 and 66 in the rafters, and the Penguins will probably address the issue when they move into their new arena in two years.

The candidates will probably come from the rosters of the 1991 and 1992 Stanley Cup champions. Ron Francis was an integral part of those teams, joining the Penguins in a stretch-run trade from Hartford in 1991. Francis was a diligent and responsible player who was also a plus in the community. But though he spent seven full seasons with the Penguins, he served 14 years with Hartford Whalers/ Carolina Hurricanes organization, and that's the franchise with which he's most closely identified.

Goalie Tom Barrasso is a candidate, too. He was something of an unsung hero on the offense-minded championship teams. Barrasso also has some sentiment for the place Pittsburgh occupied in his career. When he retired, he asked that the paperwork be manipulated with a phantom signing that allowed him to officially end his career as a member of the Penguins even though he'd finished on the St. Louis Blues' roster. The feeling wasn't always mutual, though. Barrasso's often prickly personality alienated people, and those types usually aren't singled out for number retirement ceremonies. Perhaps some of those feelings will be blunted with the passage of more time.

The most interesting candidate is Jaromir Jagr, who was drafted in time to be a member of the first Stanley Cup team. Jagr had a great career with the Penguins. Too bad it ended on such a sour note. After signing a huge contract to stay with the Penguins, Jagr wanted out, telling people he was "dying alive" with the Penguins. After a rocky stay with the Washington Capitals, Jagr seems to have found a home with the New York Rangers. Penguins fans still boo every time he touches the puck, so retiring his number probably wouldn't please the ticket buyers.

There are deserving stars from the earlier days as well (Jean Pronovost, Rick Kehoe, Syl Apps, Dave Burrows), but number retirement is usually reserved for players who were part of championship seasons.

The verdict here: Barrasso is a possibility. Otherwise,

wait until the day Sidney Crosby retires to have the next ceremony to retire a number.

WHAT IS THE PENGUINS' FOOLPROOF PLAN FOR BUILDING A WINNER?

57 The plan is this simple: Lose a lot.

The Penguins won the Stanley Cup in 1991 and 1992 because they built a foundation of talent with bad seasons that led to prime draft picks. First, the organization had the wisdom to hold onto their number-one pick, which was not always the case. The Penguins of the 1970s were forever trading top draft picks to get short-term help.

The key to the Stanley Cup championships was the horrendous 1983–1984 season that saw the Penguins set a team record with an NHL low of 38 points. In the long run, that suffering was worth it because it led to the first overall pick in the 1984 draft, Mario Lemieux. The Penguins parlayed their 16–58–6 record into a franchise player who would improve the team and dramatically boost attendance. But even with Lemieux in the fold, the Penguins still had a long way to go. They steadily got better, but still missed the playoffs in five of the next six seasons. That guaranteed them one of the top-5 choices in the draft.

The Penguins got one more superstar player out of those drafts—Jaromir Jagr, the fourth player chosen in the 1990 draft. But the others they acquired as first-round picks were then bartered in trades to fill needs. Hall of Fame defenseman Paul Coffey came from Edmonton in 1987 in a seven-player deal. The key players used to land Coffey were forward Craig Simpson (number-one choice in 1985) and defenseman Chris Joseph, who was the top pick in 1987. Goalie Tom Barrasso was acquired from Buffalo in 1988 for forward Darrin Shannon (first-round pick in 1988), and defenseman Doug Bodger, who was an extra first-round pick in 1984. The Penguins made a pivotal deal with Hartford in March of 1991 to acquire center Ron Francis and defenseman Ulf Samuelsson. Part of the price to get those players was speedy defenseman Zarley Zalapski, the first-round choice in 1986.

Here the formula seems to be working again. Hamstrung by limited funds after emerging from bankruptcy, the Penguins fell into a steady decline at the start of the new century. Those last-place finishes again translated into an excellent drafting position, although an element of luck was involved this time—the Penguins had to win the draft lottery to make center Sidney Crosby the first pick in the 2005 draft. A year earlier, they had the second spot in the draft and selected forward Evgeni Malkin. Goalie Marc-Andre Fleury was the top choice in the 2003 draft—the Penguins wound up with the number-2 spot, then traded up with Florida to take control of the first round. In 2006, forward Jordan Staal was the second player chosen after more good fortune in the lottery. The Penguins viewed Staal more as a long-range part of their plans, but were pleased to discover that he was NHL-ready as an 18-year-old.

With that nucleus of young talent, the Penguins are poised for another run as a Cup contender. So don't despair when the inevitable down cycle comes; all that losing may lead to a lot of winning later on.

DID THE PENGUINS SERIOUSLY CONSIDER TRADING THE FIRST DRAFT PICK IN 1984?

It's become popular to laud former Penguins general manager Ed Johnston for resisting offers for the number-one pick in the 1984 draft. But was Johnston really that tempted?

The Penguins worked hard to get that overall top spot, putting together a 38-point season under first-year coach

Lou Angotti. The reward for all that suffering was the first pick, and the right to select Mario Lemieux.

Just a year earlier, the Penguins had made an ill-advised deal in which they traded first-round spots with Minnesota. Pittsburgh finished dead last that year, but couldn't capitalize on that because they had to wait until the North Stars' turn came at the 15th spot in the first round. The Penguins weren't about to repeat that mistake, especially with Lemieux clearly at the head of the 1984 class.

Lemieux was considered a potential franchise player because his skill and size allowed him to dominate games. He had the same agent as Wayne Gretzky, and even wore No. 66, which was Gretzky's famous No. 99 upside down. The Pittsburgh media had even gone to Quebec during the dreary Penguins season to do stories about Lemieux's career in junior hockey.

Other teams called with tempting offers to try to get the right to pick Lemieux. The Quebec Nordiques, desperate for a French-speaking star, offered all three of the Stastny brothers. Peter Stastny was at his peak, just 27 years old, and coming off a 119-point season. He would play ten more years in the NHL, and post a pair of 100-point seasons on his way to the Hall of Fame. Anton Stastny was a worthy but lesser player. He'd scored 62 points in the previous season and would wind up playing four more years. Marian Stastny was a lesser value, age 31 and close to the end of his effectiveness. He would stay in the NHL for just two more seasons. They were good players. But none of them was a franchise player.

Minnesota general manager Lou Nanne liked publicity, so he made a show of offering the Penguins all of his draft picks for their number-one choice. It seemed like an overwhelming deal, but it really wasn't. The draft is more guesswork than science after the first two rounds. What use would the Penguins have for an extra choice in the seventh round? It was easy to turn down Minnesota.

The fact of the matter was that the Penguins' marketing department was already designing campaigns around Lemieux before the draft. The only dissent in the front office came from long-time scout Ken Schinkel, who bought into the reports that Lemieux was a "floater," a player who didn't give maximum effort at all times. The smarter decision makers rightly figured that Lemieux probably got bored at times because he was so easily dominating the Quebec Major Junior League.

When draft day rolled around, the Penguins ignored all the chatter from other teams and selected Lemieux. It was an automatic choice, and it was the pivotal moment in franchise history. None of the deals that were proposed was worth serious deliberation.

WERE THE BANKRUPT PENGUINS THE VICTIMS OF THE NHL'S WILD SPENDING?

59

The Penguins were the NHL's best team in the early 1990s, and the league's most troubled franchise by the end of that decade.

They filed for bankruptcy protection in 1998 when they were unable to pay their bills. Trouble had been building for some time, however. Back in 1995, they were so far behind on their rent at the Civic Arena that the landlord, Spectacor, considered padlocking the doors before one of their exhibition games that year.

The primary member of the nonlocal ownership group was Howard Baldwin, whose ownership took over early in the 1991–1992 season. Baldwin's past experience had been with start-up leagues such as the World Hockey Association and World Football League. Those renegade leagues rarely had the strict procedures for screening ownership candidates that established organizations such as the NFL and Major League Baseball had. Among the established leagues, the NHL was known as the most lenient in keeping tabs on owners' finances. Baldwin loved being the public face of sports teams, but he was usually managing someone else's money. Because of that, he was prone to making popular moves that weren't necessarily smart business.

After the 1991 season, Baldwin and Mario Lemieux's agents got together on a six-year, $42 million contract. It broke new ground for the NHL. Baldwin thought it was important that Lemieux have the game's best contract, since he was the NHL's best player. Part of the contract called for the Penguins to purchase Lemieux's marketing rights. Lemieux's contract swelled to as much as $10 million per year, but Baldwin was confident he could recover much of that from his 50-50 split of Lemieux's marketing potential. He envisioned turning Lemieux into a hockey version of Michael Jordan, with multiple endorsement deals from national advertisers. He didn't realize that most companies had no interest in partnering with a hockey player because of the sport's regional interest. The marketing goals went unfulfilled and the Penguins were stuck for the total tab on Lemieux.

The fatal blow to the Baldwin ownership was the NHL-engineered lockout that delayed the start of the 1994–1995 season. The absence of games crimped the Penguins' cash flow and they still had to pay Lemieux under the ridiculously generous terms of his contract. The team started making giveaway deals to shed payroll.

In 1997, Baldwin added an investor, Boston-based Roger Marino, who had no interest in being a silent partner. Marino actively shopped the Penguins to other markets, and pulled the trigger on bankruptcy proceedings. When things shook out, Baldwin and Marino were both gone. Lemieux had been deferring payments and wound up as the franchise's largest unsecured creditor. That led him to take the debt as equity in the franchise and he became the face of the Penguins ownership.

It took years to pull out of the financial mess, and the Penguins still needed the NHL's salary cap and a new arena to survive.

Although the NHL should have stepped in to keep the Penguins' spending under control, the team was not a victim of the NHL's fiscal irresponsibility. The Penguins had unrealistic projections for revenue, and Baldwin did as much as anyone to drive up the overall salary scale.

PITTSBURGH PLACES

WAS FORBES FIELD REALLY THAT GREAT?

 60

Ah, Forbes Field, home of the Pirates from 1909 until 1970. To hear some old-timers talk about the place, every day featured sunny skies, balmy breezes, great seats, and a Pirates victory.

There's no doubt Forbes Field had character. The backdrop beyond the ivy-covered outfield walls was leafy Schenley Park. While it was a cozy 300 feet down the right field line, Forbes veered out to 457 feet in left-center field. They actually parked the batting cage in center field during games, and it rarely came into play. The deep outfield also featured a couple of monuments in the field of play, and those didn't see much action either. To top it off, the big, hand-operated green scoreboard in left field was a landmark, with a giant Longines clock atop the structure.

Forbes Field favored hitters because balls fell into the gaps. In more than sixty years, it never surrendered a no-hit game. The infield was rock hard, which did help the Pirates win the World Series in 1960. A sharply hit ground ball struck a pebble and bounced wildly, hitting New York Yankees shortstop Tony Kubek in the throat. Instead of a double play, the Pirates were gifted with a rally.

But Forbes Field was far from perfect. Some of the box

seats were rickety folding chairs. The concourses were narrow and dingy. Support poles forced some spectators to crane their necks to see either the pitcher or the batter. Parking was scarce, so an industry developed among neighborhood kids who would "watch" your car for a dollar. Those who didn't think they needed that measure of security often returned to find at least one tire flattened.

The legendary left-field bleachers were a bargain, but they weren't good seats by any other means. They were uncomfortable, weathered wooden planks over concrete, and fans had to sit at an angle in order to see the pitcher's mound and home plate. The vantage point was great, however, if you wanted to study the movements of the left fielder or converse with the relief pitchers hanging out in the bullpen.

The Pirates sold Forbes Field to the University of Pittsburgh in the late 1950s, preparing for a move to a multiuse stadium to be situated on the North Side. The move was expected to take place by 1965, but constant delays pushed it back to the middle of the 1970 baseball season. In the meantime, Forbes Field fell badly into disrepair as only the most urgent maintenance was performed. A final doubleheader was played on June 28, 1970, and the park was demolished the next year to clear space for the university's expanding law school.

Although affection for Forbes developed after a couple of seasons at sterile Three Rivers stadium, the fact is that people couldn't wait to get out of Forbes and into a more modern facility. Sure, Forbes Field was a fine place in its day, but the "Field of Dreams" reputation it developed in retrospect is overblown. The legend of Forbes grew through misty memories that emphasized the quirks of the park while overlooking the flaws. Much like the love affair with Terry Bradshaw, it blossomed after people saw the mediocrity that followed.

WAS THREE RIVERS STADIUM REALLY THAT BAD?

61 People didn't really embrace Three Rivers Stadium until they could actually take it home.

At that point, after the old bowl was blown to pieces on February 11, 2001, well, then it was in high demand. People scavenged for souvenirs, and parts of the 30-year-old stadium can still be found on eBay. Seats sold for hundreds of dollars, while less impressive ephemera, such as section signs, also drew spirited bidding.

Three Rivers was conceived in the late 1950s and early 1960s, when the trend in stadiums leaned toward generic concrete venues that could house both baseball and football teams. Like the reversible belt, the concept was better in theory than in practice. Multipurpose stadiums invariably wound up serving one sport better than the other. Three Rivers was a fine football stadium about ten times a year, and a horrid baseball facility for at least 81 dates.

The Pirates originally signed off on a design with an open center field that would have provided a vista of downtown. But the Steelers didn't want to sacrifice seats for a view, so the circle was closed. Without that identifying landmark, once spectators were inside, Three Rivers didn't look much different than Cincinnati's Riverfront (network broadcasters often confused the names) or Philadelphia's Veterans Stadium.

The design of Three Rivers also included some curious choices. Prime seating space was sacrificed for the Allegheny Club, even though people who join a stadium club tend to care more about the menu, bar stock, and status than they do about having a view of the game. More seats were swallowed by an ill-conceived picnic area on the fourth level, a mistake that was eventually rectified by replacing it with revenue-generating luxury boxes. And even more space was taken up by the scoreboard, which stretched across an area that would eventually house even more luxury boxes.

The lower deck wasn't that terrible for baseball watching,

but the upper deck was a disaster. The steep seats offered a worse view than some of the rooftops across the street from Wrigley Field in Chicago. There were also too many seats, which lessened the urgency to purchase tickets in advance. Because of that, the Pirates were especially vulnerable to bad weather and disappointing seasons. Nothing sells tickets like limited availability, and Three Rivers always had plenty of seats available.

The stadium operators also underestimated Pittsburghers' legendary reluctance to cross bridges. People could see the stadium; they just couldn't always figure out how to get there. Worse, the place opened before access roads were ready, so early visitors left muttering "never again." When the roads *were* finished, traffic jams were monumental because the roads only had two lanes. It wasn't until almost 20 years after the stadium opened that the Pirates took a serious look at access problems and tried to solve them.

The place served the Steelers well, though. After having their offices downtown, practicing in South Park and playing games at Pitt Stadium, it was major progress just to have everything consolidated into one site. And the ugly green turf (really a carpet) that covered the playing surface wasn't quite the anathema to football that it was to baseball.

As a baseball park, it was as awful as another 1970s phenomenon: the leisure suit.

WHAT WILL PITTSBURGHERS MISS MOST ABOUT MELLON ARENA?

Within a couple of years the Penguins will have a state-of-the-art new arena on Fifth Avenue, and Mellon Arena will likely be demolished.

Like a lot of things in Pittsburgh, the old arena created a buzz in its time, then stayed around past its usefulness. Originally built for the Civic Light Opera, with sports as an afterthought, the big selling point was the arena's retractable dome. But that feature was disabled in order to hang a four-sided video scoreboard from the center of the roof in the late 1990s.

Minus the dome, the arena was just another building that was too small for its main purpose. But it will wind up lasting nearly 50 years, which means it will outlive Three Rivers Stadium by almost 20 years. Here's a look at the top reasons it will occupy a spot in the memories of Pittsburghers.

THE SHAPE

"The Igloo" was a natural nickname because Mellon

looked like something that had just been dropped out of an ice cream scoop. Squatty and sturdy, the roof gleamed in the sunshine and had an interesting way of shedding snow like dandruff in the winter. In aerial shots it was a shiny ladybug.

THE JIGGLE

The original seating capacity was just over 11,000. In its final days, the Penguins could cram 17,132 people in for hockey. The first major construction project was the north and south balconies, which opened in 1976. As demand for tickets increased, they started jerry-rigging extra seats in every available space. When the building is packed and the crowd is especially lively, the newly constructed areas have a disturbing tendency to sway a bit, which makes patrons want to check to see if all the construction permits were in order.

THE ORANGENESS

No matter how many seats were in the arena, it always seemed that most of them were orange. It was the predominant color in the upper reaches of the arena, even though the lower seats turned to more subdued blues and dark reds in the later years.

THE HEALTH BENEFITS

There were few escalators and elevators, so most fans got

to their seats by scaling ramps and steps. Need a cold drink? It was often a pretty good hike to the concession stands, too. And, of course, anyone taller than 5 feet 10 inches had to perform an abdominal crunch to get into a seat with limited leg room. People were a lot smaller when the arena was designed in the late 1950s.

THE HISTORY

The Beatles' only Pittsburgh appearance was there. Frank Sinatra gave concerts in the building. The last New Year's Eve show of Elvis Presley's life was performed on the stage of the Civic Arena on December 31, 1976.

Ironically, some of the biggest Penguins moments were *not* there. Mario Lemieux made his NHL debut in Boston, and the Penguins won both of their Stanley Cup championships on the road. Still, the Pittsburgh Pipers claimed the first American Basketball Association (ABA) title at the arena. The Pittsburgh Triangles won a World Team Tennis title there, and the very first Arena Bowl was held there as well.

And special credit to anyone who remembers when there was an exhibit hall underneath the stands. Sometimes hockey games and outdoor shows were held at the same time.

What tops our list? Ultimately what people will remember best—and miss the most—are the performances by the stars who were on one stage or another in the building.

ON THE AIR

WHICH PITTSBURGH ATHLETE WENT ON TO THE MOST ACCOMPLISHED BROADCASTING CAREER?

Players spend a good part of their careers being interviewed on television and radio, so it's only natural that so many of them turn to careers in broadcasting once they no longer play.

Pittsburgh once had two former Major League Baseball players serving as analysts for the radio broadcasts of the city's two major college basketball programs. Former Pirates shortstop Dick Groat still teams with Bill Hillgrove on Pitt basketball games, although ex-Pirates pitcher Nellie King is retired from his duty with Ray Goss on Duquesne broadcasts. Groat was a standout basketball player at Duke, and King fell into his job when he joined Duquesne's athletic administration after leaving the Pirates' broadcast booth in 1975.

But Pittsburgh has had more contributions to the microphone

than that. Here's a look at five former players whose careers on the air stretched outside of Pittsburgh.

5. MARK MALONE

The former Steelers quarterback (1980–1987) started at the bottom, serving as an intern for WPXI-TV. That allowed him to learn the business and progress to a role on the air. Malone then moved on to ESPN, where he grew enough to cover events outside of football. The demands of ESPN's travel schedule led him to leave for a sports anchor spot with WBBM-TV, the CBS affiliate in Chicago.

4. MERRIL HOGE

When a series of concussions forced him to retire from the NFL, Hoge became a full-time broadcaster. The former Steelers' running back (1987–1993) is a regular on ESPN's NFL shows and is often kidded by his colleagues for his ongoing loyalty to the Steelers.

3. RALPH KINER

His broadcasting career started in Pittsburgh during the 1960 World Series. WIIC (now WPXI) was looking for a former player to help with local shows wrapped around NBC's coverage of the Series. Pirates announcer Bob Prince recommended Kiner, who had been working as an executive with a minor league team in San Diego. Kiner was the Pirates' biggest drawing card through some lean years in the 1950s. The work in Pittsburgh led to a job on Chicago White Sox broadcasts in 1961. Kiner was then hired by the New York Mets and has been part of their broadcasts since the franchise's inaugural season in 1962. Although some of his malapropisms have become legendary ("On this Father's Day, we want to wish all you fathers a happy birthday"), Kiner remains an astute analyst who draws consistent praise from the tough New York columnists.

2. TERRY BRADSHAW

The uninhibited Bradshaw is a natural performer, which makes him perfect for Fox's raucous NFL pregame show. After his retirement from the Steelers, Bradshaw signed with CBS and was an analyst paired with Verne Lundquist. He moved to the studio show, and made the switch to Fox in 1994. Although his football fame made him attractive to the networks, there is now a generation of viewers with no memory of Bradshaw's 1970–1983 playing career with the Steelers that views him purely as a broadcaster.

1. JOE GARAGIOLA

Some of Garagiola's earliest comedy material came from being a member of the 1952 Pirates, who set a franchise futility record with their 42–112 record. "One day we had a rainout and we staged a victory party," was a favorite joke. Garagiola wasn't as bad of a ballplayer as he likes to portray. His career average was a respectable .257 over nine seasons with four different teams. As a broadcaster, he broke out of sports and was one of the hosts of NBC's *Today Show* from 1967 to 1973 and again in 1991–1992. Garagiola hosted five different game shows and his relationship with NBC Sports lasted nearly 30 years, including many on the network's top baseball coverage team. He handled both play-by-play and analysis for NBC. He was even the guest host of the Tonight Show on May 14, 1968, the only time any of the Beatles appeared on the show. He interviewed Paul McCartney and John Lennon. In more recent years, viewers have come to associate the old catcher with his hosting of the Westminster Kennel Club Dog Show from Madison Square Garden.

For handling early mornings, late nights, and just about everything in between, the versatile Garagiola gets the nod as Pittsburgh's most distinguished jock turned announcer.

WHICH PITTSBURGH BROADCASTER DESERVES HALL OF FAME CONSIDERATION?

 The first sports broadcast came out of Pittsburgh in 1921, when Harold Arlin described a game between the Pirates and Philadelphia Phillies for KDKA radio listeners on August 5.

Since then Pittsburgh has had a number of distinctive and original voices calling games. The best known is Myron Cope, who served as the analyst for the Steelers radio network from 1970 through 2005. Cope had been a magazine writer of some note when the Steelers had the notion to put him on the broadcasts, where his colorful personality and distinctive squawk took over. Along the way he invented the Terrible Towel, which has become a universal symbol of Pittsburgh sports fandom, a flag that has flown all over the world in support of teams wearing black and gold.

Bob Prince was the voice of the Pirates from 1954 through 1975, after spending seven years as Rosey

Rowswell's junior partner. Prince, who started in the days of tickertape re-creations of games, was a flamboyant personality who took center stage when he broadcast. He was fond of nicknaming players and using expressions to fit situations. Prince would shout, "Kiss it goodbye" when a Pirate hit a home run, and offer a mournful "Call a doctor" when an opposing player hit one in a key situation. By 1975, however, Prince had started to drift too far from the games during broadcasts, and didn't change even though he had been warned frequently. But his abrupt firing after 28 years seemed heartless to the public, and the move created a negative perception of the Pirates at a time when the Steelers were taking over the city.

Prince was a strong influence on Penguins announcer Mike Lange. When Lange arrived in Pittsburgh in 1974, Prince urged him to develop some signature phrases. Lange took the lesson to heart and expanded on what Prince had done, coming up with a list of expressions ("Great Balls of Fire," "Hallelujah Hollywood") that he still regularly drops into his broadcasts.

All three of those announcers have been recognized by their sport's Hall of Fame. Cope received the Pro Football Hall of Fame's Pete Rozelle award in 2005, Lange accepted the Hockey Hall of Fame's Foster Hewitt Memorial award in 2001, and Prince was the posthumous winner of the Ford C. Frick award from the Baseball Hall of Fame in 1986.

Yet there are others who are also worthy of recognition.

Canadian-born Joe Tucker called Steelers games for 32 seasons from 1936 to 1967, with an impressive deep voice and emotional involvement that earned him the nickname "The Screamer." Jack Fleming first joined the Steelers' radio team in 1958 as a color analyst, then succeeded Tucker on play-by-play. Fleming's no-frills approach meshed well with Myron Cope's histrionics when the two were paired up in 1970. Fleming's call of Franco Harris's 1972 "Immaculate Reception" is the perfect example of his style. He stayed on top of a complicated play, offering a vivid description with enthusiasm that never got in the way of telling the story.

But the announcer most deserving of Hall recognition is Jim Woods, who was Bob Prince's partner on Pirates games from 1957 to 1969. Nicknamed "Possum," Woods had a voice that crackled with excitement and his descriptive skills were exceptional. Pittsburgh was one stop in a career that included calling games for the New York Yankees, New York Giants, St. Louis Cardinals, Oakland Athletics, and Boston Red Sox. Woods had the talent but not the inclination to be a number-one announcer. He didn't want all the public relations responsibilities that came with that. So Woods was a solid number 2 to many Hall of Famers, including Mel Allen, Russ Hodges, Prince, and Jack Buck.

Woods, who died in 1988 at age seventy-one, deserves a plaque at Cooperstown along with the other Hall of Famers.

WHAT WERE BOB PRINCE'S BEST NICKNAMES?

Bob Prince broadcast Pirates games from 1948 until 1975, when he was heartlessly fired from the job.

Prince made no pretense of objectivity. He was a Pirate fan broadcasting for an audience of like-minded people. His play-by-play calls were filled with expressions like "Kiss it goodbye" for a Pirates home run and a smug "We had 'em all the way," which followed any victory, even those that came with significant late-inning stress. A ball in the gap that was skipping on the artificial turf at Three Rivers Stadium was "a bug on the rug" and a ball that was almost fair was foul "by a gnat's eyelash" or "close as fuzz on a tick's ear." When a double play was in order, Prince would implore the pitcher to throw a "Hoover" ball, one that would clean the bases like a vacuum cleaner might. Sure, it all may have been hokey, but it got Prince noticed. Most people loved him, some couldn't stand him, but everyone was aware of him.

A big component of Prince's style was nicknames. At times he wouldn't even use a players' proper name when he came to bat, figuring the audience knew him just as well by the other name. In tribute, here are our top-ten Prince nicknames (disclaimer: Prince didn't originate all of the nicknames. Some were started by the players, but it was through Prince's broadcasts that the public came to know them).

10. HARVEY HADDIX, "THE KITTEN"

This is one that originated with players, specifically Haddix's St. Louis teammates, who thought he bore a resemblance to the larger Harry "The Cat" Brecheen.

9. MANNY SANGUILLEN, "THE ROAD RUNNER"

This was a Prince invention, a nod to Sanguillen's speed, which was uncommon for a catcher.

8. EL ROY FACE, "THE BARON OF THE BULLPEN"

Another Prince original, this perfectly fit the confident stride Face had when he came into difficult situations as a relief pitcher.

7. BOB FRIEND, "BART"

Another Prince creation, this was a shortened form of Friend's unusual middle name of Bartmess.

6. VERNON LAW, "THE DEACON"

Law was an ordained minister in the Mormon church.

5. BILL VIRDON, "THE QUAIL"

Prince hung this on him because of Virdon's habit of getting bloop hits just over the infield. Prince called those hits "dying quails."

4. RONNIE KLINE, "THE CALLERY, P-A HUMMER"

Kline was from a small town north of Pittsburgh called Callery, and he was a power pitcher in his younger days. In the parlance of the dugouts then, a hard thrower could "hum it."

3. JIM WOODS, "THE POSSUM"

Woods was Prince's broadcast partner from 1958 to 1969 and a close friend. "Possum" actually originated with Yankees players Whitey Ford and Enos Slaughter when Woods was working games in New York. Woods got a close-cropped haircut and the players decided that style, coupled with his overbite, made him "look like a possum." Woods never minded the nickname, and there's something wonderfully bizarre about a middle-aged man routinely answering to the name "Possum."

2. DON HOAK, "THE TIGER"

This may have been given to Hoak before Pittsburgh, but Prince exploited it during Hoak's playing career and his two years in the broadcast booth (1965–1966). It fit perfectly because of Hoak's intensity. Former *Pittsburgh Press* columnist Roy McHugh wrote that Hoak always seemed to be possessed by some inner rage. The late Joe O'Toole, a longtime Pirates executive, neatly summed up Hoak's aggressive nature by saying, "He was always on the muscle."

1. PRINCE HIMSELF, "THE GUNNER"

The Pirates publicity material always explained that Prince got this name because of his rapid-fire style. In later years, Prince and Woods enjoyed finally telling the true story. Done with a spring training broadcast, Prince and Woods stopped in a bar in some small town in Florida. Prince struck up a conversation with the only other patron, a disheveled woman with matted hair, missing teeth, and tattered clothing. Her husband came in, misread Prince's intentions, and pulled out a gun. Prince talked his way out of the situation and he and Woods scrambled to their car. The next day, Woods set the starting lineup for the radio audience, then said, "and here's the Gunner," catching Prince by surprise with the inside reference.

It stuck, and the man with all the nicknames had one of his own.

WHAT WERE THE WORST IDEAS IN THE HISTORY OF PITTSBURGH SPORTS BROADCASTING?

Sometimes ideas are bold and innovative but wind up being very bad. Here are examples of some that must have made perfect sense in the conference room, but wilted badly when put into practice.

PITTSBURGH'S FIRST FEMALE SPORTSCASTER

Westinghouse Broadcasting, which owned KDKA-TV, had a good idea that it executed poorly. Westinghouse was always looking for ways to keep non-fans interested in the sports segments on the newscasts. Their choice for sports director was inspired. Bill Currie was a witty and literate son of the South who found success casting himself as a country bumpkin in the big city. Currie's nightly commentaries were often about his failed marriage, his toupee, and his wrangling with management types ("The yummies up on Carpet Corridor") more than sports. Viewers ate it up.

When casting about for a number-2 sportscaster in 1973, someone had the idea to hire Lee Arthur, an attractive female who had performed on Broadway. The hire certainly garnered a lot of attention. Today ESPN's *Sportscenter* is likely to have at least one woman anchoring, but in 1973, the idea of a woman delivering sports news was revolutionary. (Consider that when Three Rivers Stadium opened in 1970, a features reporter from the *Pittsburgh Press* was turned away from the press box because no women were permitted to work there.) Arthur didn't go into locker rooms, but her presence on the sideline became an issue when crusty Steelers equipment manager Jack Hart tried to eject her from a training camp practice field.

This was a noble experiment, but Westinghouse made the wrong choice. Arthur didn't know sports and she didn't seem to have basic reporting skills. She did an interview with Pirates infielder Rennie Stennett and asked what he planned to do when his baseball career was over. Stennett was 23 at the time. Arthur left after a couple of years on the job and was replaced by Linda Carson, whose husband, Bud, was the Steelers' defensive coordinator. Linda Carson moved over to weather duties in 1976 and KDKA-TV hasn't had a full-time female sportscaster since then.

ROCKY BLEIER, SPORTSCASTER

WPXI-TV (then known as WIIC) was consistently last in the local news ratings. What better way to improve that standing than to hire a freshly retired Super-Bowl-era Steelers player as a sports anchor? The choice was Bleier, whose recovery from Vietnam War wounds had been made into a TV movie, *Fighting Back*.

It seemed like a perfect match, an incredibly popular ex-player on a station that needed more viewers. The problem was that Bleier wasn't very good on the air. In fact, his tongue-tangled work was often cringe-inducing. There was one famous night when Bleier perfectly nailed all seven syllables of Fernando Valenzuela's name, only to report that he had pitched a "seven-hit shitout" against the Giants.

People loved Bleier when he was No. 20 for the Steelers; they weren't so crazy about watching him stumble through sportscasts on Channel 11. Bleier left when his contract expired. Ironically, he's gone on to earn a comfortable living as a motivational speaker. He lists IBM, Merrill Lynch, and Time-Warner among his clients for speeches that cost anywhere from $10,000 to $20,000. His website biography makes no mention of his time at WPXI, which probably means he didn't enjoy the experience any more than viewers did.

KURT ANGLE, SPORTSCASTER

Same theory, different address. WPGH-TV needed a weekend sportscaster and turned to Angle, the Mt. Lebanon native who had won a gold medal in wrestling at the 1996 Olympics. There was name value, certainly. But Angle had no broadcasting experience, and it showed.

Angle struggled under the best of circumstances, and fell apart if breaking news changed the script. His melt-down moment came on July 12, 1997, when Pirates pitchers Francisco Cordova and Ricardo Rincon combined on a late-ending 10-inning no-hitter against Houston at Three Rivers Stadium. Angle had to go on the air, ad lib the story, and narrate highlights on short notice. Wrestling in the Olympics was easier for him than that task was.

Angle left the station after a year. Like Bleier, though, he succeeded with another form of public speaking. Angle became a star for World Wrestling Entertainment, where a big part of his repertoire was his ability to deliver on interviews that helped sell tickets and pay-per-view orders.

ALAN CUTLER, BASEBALL ANNOUNCER

Cutler was the weekend sports anchor at KDKA-TV who worked too hard at trying to be a zany character. Someone at the station incorrectly thought he'd be a good fit on the station's Pirates telecasts, so he was made a member of the crew for the 1986 season. Cutler overwhelmed the broadcasts, had no chemistry with his boothmates, and didn't seem to know a lot about baseball. Sometime during the season he was banished from the booth and spent the rest of the year as a roving reporter, contributing occasional interviews. Not long after that badly failed experiment, the Pirates started exercising more control over the broadcasts of their games.

WHAT WAS THE BEST COMMERCIAL INVOLVING A PITTSBURGH PLAYER?

67 Success brings opportunities off the field, both locally and nationally. Players have always been drawn to endorsements because they mean extra money and often a garage full of the sponsor's product. But what was the best commercial a Steelers player ever made?

The Steelers of the 1970s were too early for the standard "I'm going to Disneyworld" commercial. Jerome Bettis and Hines Ward shared that one after Super Bowl XL. That was just one of many for Bettis, who was all over television and radio during his years with the Steelers.

There's also Hall of Fame linebacker Jack Lambert, who did a memorable local commercial for Kennywood Park, splashing his way through one ride with broadcaster Myron Cope. As for group pitchmen, Pirates fans of a certain age remember the early 1970s, when several Pirates did commercials for a bakery that allowed consumers to trade bread wrappers for tickets. Richie Hebner's Boston accent turned the wrappers into "wappers," and every kid in Pittsburgh could mimic his delivery.

The Pirates did an in-house commercial in 2005 that featured pitcher Oliver Perez baking cookies, but burning them because he had too much heat, just like his fastball. His tag line, "Oh no, I burned them again," became a catch phrase for Pirates fans.

But these all pale in comparison to the ultimate commercial, done by Steelers defensive tackle Joe Greene for Coca-Cola in 1979. In the commercial an obviously distressed Greene limps off the field with a grimace on his face and his white jersey slung over his shoulder. A small boy, played by Tommy Okon, offers Greene his bottle of Coke. Greene refuses at first, then accepts and grudgingly thanks the boy. The boy walks away, disappointed at his encounter with his hero. Meanwhile, Greene drinks the entire bottle of cola and apparently feels better. Greene then hollers to the boy, smiles broadly, and tosses him the jersey. The boy thanks him and the commercial ends with warm and fuzzy feelings. The commercial was voted one of the best ever in a *TV Guide* poll, and even led to a TV movie, *The Steeler and the Pittsburgh Kid*.

WHAT ARE THE MOST MEMORABLE CATCH-PHRASES IN PITTSBURGH SPORTS BROADCASTING?

68 Pittsburgh sports fans have always responded well to broadcasters who root for the home teams. They've had the pleasure of listening to some of the most colorful announcers in the business, including Bob Prince on baseball, Myron Cope on football, and Mike Lange on hockey. Prince was a big believer in having signature calls, and he greatly influenced Lange. Cope developed his own language speaking off the cuff on his nightly talk show, and some of the lingo spilled over to his work as the analyst on Steelers broadcasts.

Here are the top-five phrases that stuck in the minds of listeners.

5. "RAISE THE WINDOW, AUNT MINNIE," ALBERT KENNEDY "ROSEY" ROWSWELL

Rowswell was the first long-term Pirates play-by-play broadcaster, working from 1936 until his death in 1955. His exhortation to Aunt Minnie was his home run call, which was especially popular when slugger Ralph Kiner was with the Pirates. Rowswell would then have sound effects of glass shattering and follow with, "She never made it." Yes, it was hokey, but that's the way they did things then. The audience loved it.

4. "WE HAD 'EM ALL THE WAY," BOB PRINCE

This was Prince's standard signoff on any Pirates victory. It didn't matter if a one-run game had ended with the bases loaded, the Pirates had them all the way.

3. "BUY SAM A DRINK AND GET HIS DOG ONE, TOO," MIKE LANGE

Lange had two basic phrases when he came to town in 1974—"Great balls of fire" and "Hallelujah Hollywood." He constantly added to them over the years and came up with things that ranged from insipid ("Eddie Spaghetti" and "How much fried chicken can you eat?") to inspired, like this one. This has a non sequitur quality that somehow works.

2. "YOI!" MYRON COPE

This was an expression of amazement that a generation of ethnic grandmothers used. Cope started using it on the air and it fit any number of situations. "That pass was nearly intercepted. Yoi!" or "Yoi, the Browns have scored 2 touchdowns in less than three minutes to tie the game." Really severe situations call for a Double Yoi, which was also the title of Cope's autobiography.

1. "KISS IT GOODBYE," BOB PRINCE

This was his home run call and it was classic. If the blast was majestic enough, Prince would have time to stretch it out for full effect. In those cases, it was often preceded by, "You can." Important distinction: Only Pirates home runs were kissed goodbye. Opposition homers were too tragic to celebrate.

WAS A SPORTSCASTER JUSTIFIED IN SWEARING ON THE AIR AFTER THE PIRATES LOST THE 1972 PLAYOFFS?

The Pirates were defending champions in 1972, and the team appeared to be even better than the one that beat the Baltimore Orioles in the World Series the year before.

The season started a week late because of a player strike, and the Pirates needed some time to kick into high gear. Once they did, though, they sailed to their third consecutive National League East title without a serious challenge, winning the division by 11 games under first-year manager Bill Virdon.

The year was filled with greatness: Steve Blass won 19 games and Roberto Clemente doubled on September 30 for his 3,000th career hit. Five players made the National League All-Star team. The Pirates wrapped up their division on September 20, which gave them more than two weeks to prepare for the Cincinnati Reds in the playoffs.

The best-of-5 series opened in Pittsburgh with the teams splitting the first two games. The Pirates won game 3 at 3–2 behind Nelson Briles and Dave Giusti, but fell 7–1 the next day to force a fifth game. The Pirates took a 3–2 lead into the bottom of the ninth and Virdon called on Giusti to relieve Blass.

Giusti, who had allowed only three home runs in 74⅔ innings all season, hung a palm ball than Johnny Bench lined over the right field wall to tie the game. Tony Perez singled and rookie George Foster ran for him. Denis Menke followed with a single, moving Foster to second. Giusti, who had led the Pirates with 22 saves, was replaced by another right-hander, Bob Moose. Cesar Geronimo flied to center, moving Foster to third. Darrell Chaney popped out. Moose was facing pinch hitter Hal McRae, one out from forcing extra innings. He threw a pitch in the dirt that catcher Manny Sanguillen couldn't block, and Foster raced home with the winning run. The game, series, and season were over.

Pittsburgh was stunned by the ninth-inning collapse. The discussion around town had centered on whether Detroit or Oakland would be the better World Series opponent, not about the Reds. Now the Pirates were done, without a chance to defend their title.

Up at WIIC-TV (now WPXI), a young sportscaster named Jan Hutchins was assembling the highlights for the six o'clock news show. The gloomy Pirates news was the lead story on the newscast. Hutchins turned to veteran anchorman Adam Lynch in the busy newsroom and asked, "You think I could get away with saying, 'What a shitty way to lose a game' on the air?" Lynch figured Hutchins was joking and told him he thought it was appropriate for the circumstances.

The news went on the air; Hutchins showed the finish of the game and as Moose's pitch rolled away from Sanguillen, he mournfully uttered the line he had run past Lynch in the newsroom. After the newscast, station management swarmed the studio. Meetings were held and a response plan was formulated, but the fallout was negligible. No one seemed to be offended.

Even the TV critic from the *Pittsburgh Press* gave Hutchins a pass, reasoning that he had only verbalized what was on the minds of most viewers—it really was a pretty awful way to lose a game. Hutchins's comment summed that up.

ARTS AND LETTERS

WHAT WAS VINCE LASCHEID'S GREATEST HIT?

70 Vince Lascheid is best known as the answer to the ultimate cornball Pittsburgh trivia question: Who played for the Pirates, Steelers, and Penguins in the same year?

Lascheid did indeed play the organ for all three teams, although his profile was much lower at Steelers games. He made his reputation at baseball and hockey, not only leading cheers (Yes, "Let's Go Bucs" bore a startling resemblance to "Let's Go Pens") but coming up with ways to musically salute players. Lascheid's gift—beyond his musicianship—was an impish sense of humor and a willingness to take chances.

Sometimes the latter got him in trouble. The Pirates were once in frequent disagreement with umpire Frank Pulli over ball and strike calls. One day, when Pulli finally called a strike, Lascheid punctuated the moment with a sarcastic "ta-da." Pulli seethed, then had an attendant summon Lascheid to the umpire's locker room after the game, where Pulli made known his preference to work without musical accompaniment.

Some of the player salutes were obvious: Dave "Cobra" Parker got several bars of snake charmer music. Others were groan-inducing reaches. Jason Kendall was greeted with "Grease," a roundabout reference to Kendall Motor Oil.

Eventually, fully staffed "in-game entertainment" departments took over the area sports venues. Pirates players began to choose their own music, which led to the annoying snippets of hip hop that accompanied their walks to the plate. As the Pirates greatly reduced his role, Lascheid semiretired to Sunday games. As for the Penguins, they soon eliminated the organ, right after inducting Lascheid into the team's Hall of Fame.

But when he was at it full time, Lascheid delighted in coming up with songs for players on every team. In fact, Lascheid pioneered musical trash talk. Steve Garvey, the perfectly coiffed Dodgers first baseman with the crisp uniform, always got "There She Is, Miss America." When pint-sized Dennis Polonich was stirring things up for the Detroit Red Wings, Lascheid's putdown was Randy Newman's "Short People."

There were two serenades in which Lascheid took particular pride. One debuted in 1980, when Pete Rose joined the Philadelphia Phillies after leaving the Cincinnati Reds. At that time, free agency was still relatively new, and it was jarring to see familiar players in new uniforms. Lascheid came up with the perfect musical statement, playing "Second Hand Rose" the first time Rose stepped into the batters box for the Phillies.

But his all-time best had come months earlier during the 1979 World Series. It was so clever it attracted the attention of the national press corps. The visiting Baltimore Orioles had an outfielder named Benny Ayala. In the hands of a lesser tunesmith, perhaps Elton John's "Bennie and the Jets" would have sufficed. But that wasn't good enough for Laschied, whose serious jazz chops had led him to tour with Tex Beneke in the big-band era. No, Lascheid was able to dig a little deeper and come up with the selection that would epitomize his pun-loving personality. He played Benny Ayala on with "Tie (Ayala) Ribbon 'Round the Old Oak Tree."

WHAT WAS THE BEST PITTSBURGH SPORTS MOVIE?

71 The three professional teams have all been part of major motion pictures, and Pittsburgh even got a fictional basketball franchise in another movie. The films had varying degrees of quality, box office success, and Pittsburgh scenery over a span of more than 30 years. There have been plenty of bit parts: The Pirates make a cameo appearance in the original 1967 *The Odd Couple* as Bill Mazeroski hits into a triple play against the New York Mets at Shea Stadium. The Steelers are one of the Super Bowl teams in *Black Sunday*, a thriller that features a killer blimp hovering over the stadium. Terry Bradshaw appeared in several movies with Burt Reynolds in the 1970s and recently revived his film career with a nude scene in 2006's *Failure to Launch*.

Rather than focusing on bit parts and cameos, though, these are the movies most likely to connect with Pittsburgh sports fans.

5. "SUDDEN DEATH," 1995

Much of this was filmed at Mellon Arena during the 1994 NHL labor lockout. Howard Baldwin, who owned part of the Penguins then, was one of the producers, and his wife Karen came up with the hockey-centric plot. Jean-Claude Van Damme played a fire inspector whose career took a downward turn after he failed to rescue a child from a burning building. But Van Damme was the point man in trying to foil a plot to blow up the arena during game seven of the Stanley Cup finals, with the vice president of the United States in attendance. "Terror goes into overtime" was one the lines used to promote the movie. It was formula stuff that one critic dismissed as "'Die Hard' with hockey." Minor league players wore the uniforms of the Penguins and Chicago Blackhawks for the on-ice sequences. Powers Booth played the villain, and Pittsburgh's favorite anthem singer, Jeff Jimerson, performed his specialty. Penguins announcers Mike Lange and Paul Steigerwald also had parts. The movie did less business than expected and contributed to Van Damme's late-1990s career slump.

4. "THE FISH THAT SAVED PITTSBURGH," 1979

This silly story also used Mellon Arena as a backdrop. It was home of the mythical Pittsburgh Pythons, a down-and-out basketball team. Enter astrologist Mona Mondieu (Stockard Channing), who determined that success was just a matter of getting players who shared the proper zodiac sign. The revamped team, Pittsburgh Pisces, enjoyed great success because the stars were in alignment, especially when the arena roof opened. Julius Erving starred and a bevy of NBA players, including Kareem Abdul-Jabbar and Duquesne's Norm Nixon, showed up. Jonathan Winters and Flip Wilson were part of the cast, too. The movie had a snappy soundtrack, thanks to Thom Bell, who was producing the Spinners' hits back then. One reviewer called it "so bad it's good," which is a nice way to sum it up. Trivia note: The part of Mona was originally supposed to go to Cher, but she was unable to fit the shooting into her schedule.

3. "ALL THE RIGHT MOVES," 1983

This technically isn't a Pittsburgh movie, but the theme of high school football in depressed mill towns resonates throughout western Pennsylvania. Tom Cruise was a high school quarterback with the requisite ethnic name of Stefen Djordjevic. He saw football as his opportunity to escape his gloomy home town. His coach, Craig T. Nelson, was also aiming for a way out, hoping to land a job as a college assistant coach. Their conflict was central to the plot. The fictional town of Ampipe was named after the American Pipe and Steel Company, the town's big employer. That's based on the real-life town of Ambridge, which took its name from the American Bridge Company. Don Yannessa, a legendary high school coach at Aliquippa, Baldwin, and Ambridge, was the technical advisor and had a small role in the film. Roger Ebert's review contained a sentence that was almost as long as the movie: "After all the junk high school movies in which kids chop each other up, seduce the French teacher and visit whorehouses in Mexico, it is so wonderful to see a movie again that remembers that most teenagers are vulnerable, unsure, sincere and fundamentally decent." Trivia note: The cast list included a character identified as "Drunk in Bar," which seems about right.

2. "FIGHTING BACK," 1980

Steelers running back Rocky Bleier's story of perseverance was a movie waiting to happen, and ABC made this one for TV at the height of the Steelers' fame as Super Bowl champions. Bleier went to Notre Dame, was drafted by the Steelers, then somehow ran afoul of his local draft board and wound up serving in Vietnam. He was wounded in combat and told he had no chance to resume his career. The Steelers kept him around, and Bleier worked through agonizing pain to make himself into a NFL running back. Robert Urich played Bleier and Bonnie Bedelia played his wife, Aleta. Art Carney played Steelers founder Art Rooney Sr., who always identified Carney as "the guy in the sewer," from his portrayal as Ed Norton in *The Honeymooners*. Trivia note: Richard Herd, who played Chuck Noll, went on to a recurring role in *Seinfeld* as Mr. Wilhelm, one of George Costanza's bosses with the New York Yankees.

1. "ANGELS IN THE OUTFIELD," 1951

Forbes Field is one of the stars of this charming movie. Paul Douglas plays the gruff manager of the Pirates, who was known for his terrible temper and a bad team that gave him plenty of reason to get angry. Janet Leigh was a newspaper reporter who was appalled when she overheard his language. One of the Pirates' most loyal fans was a little girl from an orphanage, who visited Forbes Field for a game and saw angels near all the players. The manager initially had no time for such nonsense, but became convinced that a higher power was helping the Pirates finally win games. Ultimately his flinty heart was melted by the little girl (Donna Corcoran). Disney did a remake of this story in 1994 with Danny Glover and Tony Danza, but it doesn't come close to matching the quality of the original. Bing Crosby, who was part of the Pirates' ownership group, makes a cameo appearance. Trivia note: Watch for two actresses who would later become famous for their work in TV series. Ellen Corby, who plays Sister Veronica, would go on to portray the grandmother on *The Waltons*. Barbara Billingsley, who is cast as a hat check girl, was a few years away from her role as June Cleaver on *Leave it to Beaver*.

WHO WINS THE BATTLE OF THE HITS?

Fight songs are a big part of college football, but not necessarily pro sports. But Pittsburgh's two most-storied professional teams have been associated with specific tunes over the years.

Anytime a team is successful, musicians head to the studio and try to create a novelty song that will gain radio airplay and be the one that becomes most closely associated with the team. Many are recorded, but few ever stick. The Pirates and Steelers have each had two songs that have endured. Here's how they stack up.

72 WHAT'S THE BEST STEELERS SONG: "Steelers Polka" by Jimmy Pol with the Frank Kalic Orchestra or "Here We Go" by Roger Wood and the Fan Club

Pol (Jimmy Psihoulis) was a radio station owner who jumped on the Steelers bandwagon early. His first version of the "Polka" came out in 1973 and was quickly released by retail giant National Record Mart on its seldom-used in-house label. The tune is "The Pennsylvania Polka" with lyrics about the Steelers. Much of the original was dedicated to Franco Harris, who was the team's biggest star in those days ("He's rookie of the year/We're so glad he's playing here.") The words were updated many times over the years to reflect personnel changes. The production is snappy. Kalic's tight band sounds like every western Pennsylvania wedding band, all of which have a few polkas in their repertoire. Pol has a slightly flat everyman quality that makes people feel comfortable about singing along.

There were many challengers over the years, but none was significant until Wood cut "Here We Go" for the first time in 1995. The song features a bass line so strong you can hang laundry on it. It should be used to test the woofers anytime someone is contemplating a purchase of new speakers. Like "Polka," the lyrics also highlight individual Steelers and have been changed to reflect roster turnover.

207

The "Polka" is still great fun and guaranteed to get people out of their chairs as soon as they hear the first few notes. But "Here We Go" is the one that will still be playing in your head four months after football season ends. It's insidious. Songwriters are always looking for the "hook" that sticks with listeners, and Wood was Captain Hook on this one.

WHAT'S THE BEST PIRATES SONG: "Beat 'Em Bucs" by Benny Benack and the Orchestra or "We Are Family" by Sister Sledge?

Benack was a local musician who was often booked to play at Forbes Field. That ultimately created some conflict, because Roberto Clemente was convinced the Pirates lost when Benack and his band were on hand. Clemente took the concept of jinxes seriously. But how could Benny Benack be bad luck with all the spins this record got as the Pirates went on to win the 1960 World Series? The song is a bright Dixieland version of "Camptown Races" with Pirates lyrics. Local musician Joe Negri and Si Bloom each took a writing credit, but they obviously didn't spend a lot of time agonizing over this one. The lyrics are "The Bucs are going all the way," and "Beat 'em Bucs." Repeat often. It didn't have to be "American Pie." People loved it and it's associated with the 1960 team, the most beloved group of

Pirates in team history.

"We Are Family" is unique here because it's the only nationally released record that became associated with a Pittsburgh team. Sister Sledge, a four-woman group from Philadelphia, charted with this in 1979. Pirates captain Willie Stargell heard it playing on the PA system in St. Louis and told team publicist Joe Safety to get a copy to play in Pittsburgh. Stargell first joined the Pirates in 1962 and embraced the idea of the team as family—never mind that the Sledge sisters were singing, "I got all my sisters with me." The record became the Pirates anthem throughout the 1979 season, right through the World Series.

While "We Are Family" is a fine record, it never really had an intended meaning to the Pirates. It was about female unity; it was done by a group from Philadelphia and essentially hijacked from a team in St. Louis. So the pick is the unpolished jubilation of "Beat 'Em Bucs," a two-minute slice of sunshine that recalls much happier days at the old ballpark.

WHAT ARE THE FIVE BEST BOOKS ABOUT PITTSBURGH SPORTS?

74 You can not only fill a bookshelf with books pertaining to Pittsburgh sports, you can fill an entire section of a library.

The Pirates and Steelers are most heavily represented, befitting their tenure and success. There are multiple team histories of the Pirates, including those by historian John McCollister and Pittsburgh columnist Bob Smizik. Author Lou Sahadi chronicled the 1979 championship season, and Kip Richeal (*Still Walking Tall*) detailed the Pirates' transformation from 1980s doormats to a division-winning team in 1991. Willie Stargell cooperated on a disappointing ghostwritten autobiography. Al Oliver also delivered an unsatisfying autobiography. John T. Bird wrote an interesting book mostly about Bill Mazeroski that also includes profiles of other Pirates from that era. Phil Musick wrote a biography of Roberto Clemente. Former Pittsburgh columnist Bill Christine once attempted to tackle a biography of Bob Prince but, alas, it was never completed.

Former newspaperman Jim O'Brien has published more than a dozen books, most about the Steelers and Pirates, in his unique stream-of-consciousness style. Others who tackled the football team: newspaper beat writers Ed Bouchette and Jim Wexell have each done a couple of Steelers books, and longtime reporter Norm Vargo wrote one, too. The Steelers' official history was done by magazine writer Abby Mendelson. Steelers Terry Bradshaw and Jerome Bettis have autobiographies, and former linebacker Andy Russell penned two volumes of especially interesting memoirs. Broadcaster Joe Tucker wrote a history of the Steelers' early years that is now almost impossible to find.

Tom McMillan, now a Penguins executive, did an interesting informal history of the Penguins that was published in the early 1990s and is worth seeking out. Beat writer Dave Molinari did a book on the team's second Stanley Cup run and columnist Joe Starkey authored an interesting anecdotal collection, *Tales from the Pittsburgh Penguins*. Mario Lemieux and Jaromir Jagr have been the subjects of biographies, and Canadian journalist Shawna Richer covered Sidney Crosby's rookie season.

There are a lot of great stories to tell about Pittsburgh sports, and following is a look at the top-five volumes that should be on any Pittsburgh fan's shelf.

5. "OUT OF LEFT FIELD," BOB ADELMAN AND SUSAN HALL

As compelling as it is shocking, this one caused a panic in

the Pirates offices when it was published in 1976. The Pirates had granted access to Adelman and Hall, believing their efforts to chronicle Stargell's 1973 season would be something children could read. Instead, the book was almost marketed in a plain brown wrapper. The text contains transcripts of interviews conducted with players, wives, and a groupie who seemed to be on a first-name basis with about half the National League. Baseball may be the metaphor for America that George Will thinks it is, but a lot of baseball players have led interesting lives away from the field. This offers some insights into that aspect.

4. "CLEMENTE: THE PASSION AND GRACE OF BASEBALL'S LAST HERO," DAVID MARANISS

This 2006 book has the advantage of the perspective that comes with distance. It was published 33 years after Clemente's death and 32 years after the last biography of him hit the market. Maraniss does extensive research and writes superbly, so this is just as good as his biography of legendary football coach Vince Lombardi. This is the definitive Clemente book.

3. "DOCK ELLIS IN THE COUNTRY OF BASEBALL," DONALD HALL

Leave it to Ellis to have his biography written by a poet. Hall did an outstanding job writing, researching, and, perhaps most important, understanding Ellis's often outlandish personality. A lesser writer would have been easily sidetracked by Ellis's bluster. Hall provides a balanced look at a unique baseball character.

2. "DOUBLE YOI," MYRON COPE

Cope resisted efforts to write again, convinced that years of broadcast work had dulled his writing skills. Thankfully, he was wrong. Former *Pittsburgh Press* sports editor Roy McHugh helped tighten this into an entertaining memoir that is filled with Cope's wit. (Cope's previous books are also worth seeking out, even though they're not exclusively about Pittsburgh topics. *The Game That Was* is an oral history of early pro football, and *Broken Cigars* is a collection of Cope's magazine profiles, including the famous *Sports Illustrated* story about Clemente's aches and pains.)

1. "ABOUT THREE BRICKS SHY OF A LOAD," ROY BLOUNT

Blount was a *Sports Illustrated* staff writer when he got the assignment to spend the 1973 season loafing (Pittsburgh term) with the Steelers. The result is this book, which sets the standard for Pittsburgh sports literature. Blount is a gifted writer with a keen eye for detail who had total access to the Steelers players on and off the field for an entire year. It's the last season before the first championship and major players such as Jack Lambert and Mike

Webster are not yet on the scene. It's still worth reading for Blount's insights into the dichotomy of living a normal life apart from the violence on the field, as well as his take on the unique personalities that were allowed to blossom in the Steelers' relaxed atmosphere. Blount did an update after the Steelers won the Super Bowls, but any edition of this book is a good starting point.

PITTSBURGH
PEOPLE

WHAT WERE PITTSBURGH'S MOST FAMOUS FAMILY FEUDS?

Running a sports franchise is a high-pressure job, often handled by people with supreme self-confidence in their ideas. That can lead to clashes of philosophy that do more damage to an organization than any opponent could cause.

There have been intramural battles from time to time in the front offices of all the pro franchises in Pittsburgh. Here's a look at some of the most famous.

5. COACH ED JOHNSTON VS. GENERAL MANAGER BAZ BASTIEN, PENGUINS

Johnston was the coach who wanted to be general manager in 1983. He didn't have much regard for Bastien, a hockey lifer who had spent most of his career in the minor leagues. Johnston thought Bastien was behind the times at a point when the NHL was becoming more sophisticated in scouting opponents and using videotapes to instruct players. When the Penguins did little before the trading deadline and limped to the finish line in a sour season, Johnston was openly critical of Bastien. Tragedy settled the issue. Bastien was killed in a highway crash as he drove home from a banquet on March 15, 1983. The Penguins promoted Johnston to general manager only after making an offer to Bob McCammon, who used it as leverage for a new contract with the Philadelphia Flyers. Johnston acquired a lot of talent as general manager, but the Penguins failed to make the playoffs under his leadership. He was demoted and replaced by Tony Esposito on April 14, 1988.

4. MANAGER JIM LEYLAND VS. GENERAL MANAGER TED SIMMONS, PIRATES

Leyland was old-school baseball, a longtime minor leaguer with an endless supply of stories from his days of scrapping through the bush leagues for little money. Simmons was a 1960s hippie who had been a star in the major leagues and was fond of quoting *Star Wars*. The personality gulf was considerable, but it's not uncommon for people with a single purpose to work harmoniously. Not in this case, though.

Leyland's success with the Pirates had earned him a measure of respect from ownership that wasn't afforded to most managers. The Pirates never considered Leyland disposable in the manner that some organizations see their managers. Simmons wanted a more traditional chain

217

of command and provoked some clashes with Leyland over relatively minor issues. The ill will was exacerbated by ownership-mandated budget slashing. Leyland saw good players being traded for prospects, and didn't like it. The styles of the two men were incompatible. When Simmons suffered a heart attack at work, team president Mark Sauer crafted the perfect diplomatic resolution to the friction between Leyland and Simmons. He suggested Simmons announce his resignation for health reasons, which he did on June 19, 1983.

3. ART ROONEY JR. VS. DAN ROONEY, STEELERS

Steelers founder Art Rooney Sr. had career plans in mind for each of his sons, and none of them included football. For example, Rooney Sr. saw eldest son Dan as an electrician. But Dan was involved in the Steelers from the time he served as a teenage water boy at training camp. He took over running the franchise in 1969 and his brother Art Jr. took charge of the scouting department. The Steelers then built a Super Bowl dynasty through the draft, making the Rooneys the ultimate family business. Things soured in the mid-1980s, though, and Dan Rooney fired his brother after disagreements over authority. Art Rooney Jr. maintained an ownership stake in the Steelers, but no longer had a say in the operation of the team. Dan Rooney was elected to the Pro Football Hall of Fame in 2000, following his father, who was in the Hall's 1964 class. Art Rooney Jr.'s name was placed on the ballot in 2006.

2. GENERAL MANAGER SYD THRIFT VS. PIRATES OWNERSHIP

When new ownership took over the Pirates shortly after the 1985 season, they shocked baseball by hiring Thrift, a former scout who had been out of baseball for a decade. Thrift had been one of the minds behind the Kansas City Royals' innovative Baseball Academy and had unconventional ideas that impressed the Pirates. Thrift had a golden touch. He started by hiring Jim Leyland to manage the team. Then he made a series of trades that sent away veterans such as Tony Pena and Rick Rhoden and brought Doug Drabek, Bobby Bonilla, Andy Van Slyke, and other young players of considerable promise. The Pirates, who lost 104 games in 1985, were 85–75 just two seasons later. As he made one good move after another, Thrift couldn't resist calling attention to his accomplishments. A man of ample proportions, he had an ego to match. The Pirates were owned by a public-private coalition and most of their executives were industry barons who were unaccustomed to employees behaving as Thrift did. They were also upset that Thrift didn't keep them in the loop about his plans. The truth was, Thrift saw no reason to brief them because he didn't believe they had enough baseball knowledge to offer any helpful input. The relationship deteriorated and

219

Thrift was in trouble, despite his success in turning around the Pirates. Speculating on the possibility of his ouster, Thrift said, "It would be like Wayne Gretzky leaving Canada." But it happened. Thrift was fired immediately after the 1988 season, and the Pirates haven't had a general manager match his success since then.

1. BILL COWHER VS. TOM DONAHOE, STEELERS

This was the main event, a heavyweight clash of two head-strong men who wanted autonomy. Cowher was the Steelers' coach and Donahoe was the team's director of football operations. Both had volatile personalities. Cowher's sideline rants were regularly picked up by TV cameras. He was so hard to work for that assistants sometimes made lateral moves out of Pittsburgh to get into a more stable setting. One former assistant reported that Cowher would curse at his coaches through the headset when a play didn't work.

Donahoe, also mercurial, was well known for poking his head in the door of the Steelers' media room at Three Rivers Stadium to register the most peevish complaints about coverage of the team. When several assistant coaches were fired, he eschewed diplomacy and told a TV interviewer, "Those guys couldn't coach." So he not only took their jobs away, he buried their careers, too. Donahoe also made waves in the front office—he enraged some long-time Steelers staffers by firing darts at legendary coach Chuck Noll behind the scenes.

Donahoe wanted a bigger role in the organization, and he got it when Noll retired: He became director of football operations. Ultimately, though, he and Cowher began to disagree on personnel issues and less important matters. They reached a point where they rarely spoke. When Dan Rooney was later reflecting on the decision to let Rod Woodson leave as a free agent, he said it was cemented when both Cowher and Donahoe thought it was the right move. "Those guys never agreed on anything," Rooney said. Joking aside, he knew that the organization couldn't run with the top-two football men at odds. A decision had to be made. Initially it looked as though the Steelers planned to keep Donahoe. Defensive coordinator Jim Haslett was alerted to stay in town for a news conference that would introduce him as the new head coach. But late in a tumultuous week, the Steelers decided to stay with Cowher, apparently in the belief it would be easier to find a new executive than a head coach. In February of 2000, Kevin Colbert replaced Donahoe, and he and Cowher worked smoothly together, culminating with the Steelers' victory in Super Bowl XL on February 5, 2006. Donahoe moved on to Buffalo, where he had limited success.

WHO WERE PITTSBURGH'S MOST FAMOUS SPORTS COUPLES?

76 It's a cliché that the star athlete always winds up married to the prettiest cheerleader. There are times, though, when that scenario comes to life.

There have been a handful of Pittsburgh athletes over the years who have been married to women at least as famous as they are. Charlie Simmer, who played 50 games for the Penguins in 1987–1988, was married to Terri Welles, who was Playboy's Playmate of the Year in 1981. Another short-term Penguins player, Ron Duguay, was married to supermodel Kim Alexis, who appeared on 500 magazine covers and was featured in six different *Sports Illustrated* swimsuit issues. Linda Carson, who was married to Steelers defensive coordinator Bud Carson in the 1970s, spent time as a sports reporter for KDKA-TV in Pittsburgh and was later the station's weekend weather forecaster. Linda Carson also worked in television in several cites where her husband coached. But these couples, notable as they are, fail to make the cut for our top five, who are:

5. RUSS ANDERSON, PENGUINS, MARRIED TO DOROTHY BENHAM

Anderson was a standout defenseman at the University of Minnesota and the Penguins' number-2 draft pick in June of 1975. Two summers later, his fiancée, Dorothy Benham, won the Miss America competition, singing an opera selection for the talent portion of the contest. Anderson was traded to Hartford in 1981 and the couple later divorced.

4. KRIS BENSON, PIRATES, MARRIED TO ANNA BENSON

Anna Benson is the only spouse on this list who wasn't well-known before she married an athlete. She quickly made up for that with an outrageous personality that made her one of Howard Stern's preferred guests. In one interview, she promised to bed the entire team as revenge if she ever caught Kris being unfaithful. Anna Benson achieved greater notoriety after Kris was traded to the Mets during the 2004 season and her exploits became fodder for the New York gossip columns. A now-defunct magazine, *FHM*, twice had Anna Benson on its list of sexiest women in the world. Anna, who describes herself as "an irreverent humanitarian," makes no secret she was working as an exotic dancer before she met Kris. She promotes her various enterprises through a website that includes the obscenity-laden letters she's sent to public figures, including liberal filmmaker Michael Moore. Even

Anna's charity work comes with some controversy. She and Kris appeared as Santa and Mrs. Claus for a benefit in New York. Anna's skimpy red and white suit caused a stir and was another in a long line of reasons the Mets were relieved to trade Kris to the Orioles.

3. DON HOAK, PIRATES, MARRIED JILL COREY

Born Norma Jean Speranza in the coal-mining town of Avonmore, Pennsylvania, Jill Corey was signed to Columbia Records as a 17-year-old in 1952. She appeared on the cover of *Life* magazine, sang on the *Ed Sullivan Show*, and was the last featured singer on *Your Hit Parade*. She gave up her career when she married Hoak in 1961. After his playing days ended in 1964, Hoak spent two years as a Pirates broadcaster, then managed in the minor leagues. He died of a heart attack on October 9, 1969, hours after learning he did not get the Pirates' managing job. Corey went back to show business, has appeared on Broadway, and returned to the recording studio.

2. RALPH KINER, PIRATES, MARRIED NANCY CHAFFEE

Nancy Chaffee was once the fourth-ranked tennis player in the world. She played on the men's team at Southern California because the university didn't have a women's team in those days. She and Kiner were married on

October 13, 1951, and divorced in 1968. Their marriage produced a daughter and two sons, one of whom played minor league baseball. After two years of lessons, Kiner said he was finally able to beat Chaffee at tennis. Of course, he added the disclaimer that she was two weeks away from giving birth to their first child at the time.

1. TERRY BRADSHAW, STEELERS, MARRIED JOJO STARBUCK

This appeared to be a marriage made for *People* magazine—the blonde Super Bowl quarterback and the pixyish and equally blonde figure skater. Alicia "JoJo" Starbuck was well known for her skating accomplishments with partner Kenneth Shelley. They won the gold medal in pairs at the U.S. Figure Skating Championships three times between 1970 and 1972. They were also in the Olympics in 1968 and 1972. Bradshaw was coming off an 18-month marriage to another celebrity, Melissa Babish, a western Pennsylvania native who was Miss Teenage America. Bradshaw wed Starbuck in 1976 and they were married through 1983.

"I got married the first time strictly because I was depressed," Bradshaw once told ESPN. "I got married the second time because I was madly in love with my wife. She didn't love me, and she left me." It was a sad ending to what appeared to be a storybook union. The Bradshaw-Starbuck union generated the most national attention, so it tops the list.

WHO IS PITTSBURGH'S GREATEST SPORTS CHARACTER?

77 There's never been a shortage of eccentrics on the Pittsburgh sports scene. Whether they're amateur statisticians or talk show callers, they've been persistent enough to carve out a place in Pittsburgh sports lore. And we're just talking about unrelated folks, leaving out people who have some sort of official connection, like longtime Pirates equipment manager John (Hoolie) Hallahan, who was fond of speaking Pig Latin. This always baffled his young helpers, whom he would invariably address as "Jock Strap" and "Sweat Sock."

Instead we're talking about the people who worked their way to our lineup through sheer force of will. They made a name for themselves, even if it wasn't always their given name.

5. ZIVKO KOVALCHIK, TALK SHOW CALLER

Zivko's schtick was casting himself as the ultimate ethnic Pittsburgher, placing his calls to Myron Cope's talk show from the South Side Moose hall. Reality? "Zivko" was Jerry

Finn, a successful businessman who lived in Pittsburgh's Squirrel Hill section. But he had the act down, and a lot of people believed he was a tried and true South Sider, chasing shots of Imperial whiskey with Iron City beer. Finn borrowed the "Zivko" name from a professional wrestler who had worked in Pittsburgh in the 1960s. He eventually branched out and called other shows, but he made his reputation through his byplay with Cope.

4. MAURICE "MOSSIE" MURPHY, FAN, DUQUESNE BASKETBALL

By day, Maurice Murphy was a well-connected political consultant who counted the Pennsylvania State Democratic Committee among his clients. By night, though, he was the number-one cheerleader for Duquesne, a role he'd adopted when he was a student at the university. Murphy had an elaborate cheer that built slowly with cries of, "shoo shoo...rah rah..." then finished with a lively chant of "Let's Go Du-kane." Murphy would clap and bounce on the bleachers and the crowd never failed to react. A man of modest height who was a bit portly, Murphy bore at least a slight resemblance to the *Animal House* era John Belushi. Duquesne inducted him into the school's Hall of Fame in the builder category in 1993.

3. "TIGER PAUL" AUSLANDER, CHEERLEADER, PITT BASKETBALL

Paul Auslander was a Pittsburgh native whose zeal for playing sports exceeded his ability. His constant effort to play scholastic football drew the sarcastic nickname "Tiger Paul," which Auslander turned into a positive as a fan. He would run up and down the length of the basketball court, then jump and clap and exhort the fans to cheer for the Panthers. The intensity he brought to the job was obvious. Tiger Paul was so good that he was often the object of protest from the cheerleaders, who resented being upstaged. Fans loved Tiger, though, because his raw emotion came with a lack of inhibitions. Sometimes he wore a tuxedo, but he also prowled the sidelines in pajamas. His reputation led the Pirates to hire him for a brief time in the mid-1970s to lead cheers from the roof of the dugout. Ted Turner spotted him in 1976 and wanted to take him to Atlanta to cheer for the Braves. That dream didn't materialize, though, and he died in Reno, Nevada, at age 48 in February of 1992.

2. LAWRENCE "DEUCE" SKURCENSKI, STATISTICIAN, HIGH SCHOOL SPORTS

Anyone who has attended a high school basketball game anywhere in western Pennsylvania has probably seen Deuce, who delights in keeping stats even on himself. Entering the 2006–2007 season, he claimed to have seen

2,988 football games and 9,017 basketball games. Because his lingo is out of a 1950s sports section, many of those 12,000 games have been "smokin' frays." Deuce started tracking numbers at age 13 and has never stopped. His idea of heaven on earth is tournament time, when he can catch as many as eight games in two days and nights. An independent filmmaker has been working on a feature that showcases Deuce and his unique passion.

1. RADIO RICH, GENERAL HELPER, VARIOUS BROADCAST BOOTHS

Richard Glowczewski's life started out tough. He grew up in an orphanage, had a slight learning disability, and was painfully shy. He was fascinated by sports, though, and would spend his evenings dialing up games from across the country on his radio. Somehow Pirates broadcaster Bob Prince became aware of him, and Prince created a job for him as an all-around helper in the late 1950s. Because his last name was so hard to spell and pronounce, Prince started calling him Radio Rich. Rich's duties included keeping track of out-of-town scores, confirming official scoring calls with the press box, and chasing down drinks for Prince and his broadcast partners. In return Rich got a stipend from Prince, a season media credential from every team in town, and a measure of fame from Prince's on-air references to him. He continued to work as a dishwasher at the Roosevelt Hotel until automation eventually ended that job. At that point, Prince set up a corporation that allowed Rich to work for various broadcasters and teams in town. When that fell apart, Rich landed a job in the Allegheny County parks department. Through all the changes, he continued to attend games, puffing on his pipe and saying little, and living at the YMCA. Rich took a Greyhound bus trip to Chicago every summer to spend a week watching the White Sox. Thanks to Prince, Rich was treated like a VIP in the White Sox press box. Rich died in 1986, the same year that Prince succumbed to cancer.

Radio Rich was more than Pittsburgh's greatest sports character. He was also a monument to the benevolence of another unique character, Bob Prince.

WHO HAD THE CAREERS THAT MADE YOU SAY, "IS THAT ALL THERE IS?"

78 Today's clean-up hitter becomes tomorrow's utility player. That is, sometimes a career starts impressively but just doesn't last. Here are the biggest once-promising careers in Pittsburgh sports that ended in disappointment.

5. ZARLEY ZALAPSKI, PENGUINS

Zalapski was the fourth player taken in the 1986 draft, a swift-skating defenseman who could contribute offensively and quarterback the power play. He was projected to be the next Paul Coffey. But he had another "z" in his profile. He tended to zone out at times and play horrendously. Those lapses of concentration kept him from being the force he might have been.

The Penguins traded Zalapski in his fourth season, part of the price required to get Ron Francis and Ulf Samuelsson from Hartford for the 1991 playoff drive. Zalapski had 65 points for the Whalers, his best NHL season. He also played with Calgary and Montreal before finishing as a full-time NHL player in the 1997–1998 season. Aside from 12 games with Philadelphia in 1999–2000, the rest of Zalapski's career was spent in the minor leagues or Europe.

4 AMOS ZEREOUE, STEELERS

Zereoue left West Virginia a year early after setting the university's career rushing record of 4,086 yards, which included 1,589 yards in 1997. The Steelers drafted him on the third round in 1999, hoping his quick and elusive style would provide a good contrast to Jerome Bettis's bruising approach. Zereoue was with the Steelers from 1999 to 2003 and was chosen to start over Bettis in 2003. Six games later, Bettis reclaimed the starting job and Zereoue became a third-down specialist. (The Steelers were having offensive line problems and the coaching staff believed they needed a big back who could gain yards on his own.) Zereoue went to the Oakland Raiders, but didn't hold a starting job there, either. His sometimes lackadaisical approach to practice didn't win him favor with coaches.

3. BOB BAILEY, PIRATES

Signed out of a California high school for a record $150,000 bonus in 1961 (just under $1 million in 2007 dollars), Bailey was in Pittsburgh after just one season in the minor leagues. The Pirates traded veteran Don Hoak to open third base for Bailey in 1963. He responded with a .228 average, 12 home runs, and 45 RBIs at age 21. He was better the next season (.281, 11 home runs, 51 RBIs), but Bailey was never the star the Pirates thought they had discovered. Bailey was traded to the Los Angeles Dodgers for Maury Wills after the 1966 season. He played with six teams and lasted 17 years. His career average was .257 with 189 home runs and 773 RBIs. It was a respectable career, but that wasn't the level the Pirates had in mind when they lavished the bonus on him.

2. BARRY FOSTER. STEELERS

Drafted in the fifth round in 1990, Foster was a starter in his third season and set a Steelers record with 1,690 rushing yards. His twelve 100-yard games were also a record, and he was named to the Pro Bowl. Injuries limited him to 711 yards in 1993, and he ran for 851 yards in eleven games in 1994. He signed with Carolina in 1995 but failed the physical. He later signed with Cincinnati, but retired without ever playing a game for the Bengals. In five seasons, Foster played 62 games and rushed for 3,943 yards, an average of 4.3 yards per carry. The Steelers were convinced his desire never matched his considerable talent, and his career course supports that theory.

1. BOB ROBERTSON, PIRATES

This muscular redheaded slugger looked like the perfect right-handed hitting complement to the left-handed bats of Willie Stargell and Al Oliver in the Pirates lineup. Robertson was a three-time home run champion in the minor leagues and broke in as a regular player with the Pirates in 1970. He hit .287 with 27 home runs and 82 RBIs. He then batted .271 with 26 homers and 72 RBIs in 1971 as the Pirates went on to win the World Series. He slugged four home runs in the National League playoffs and two more in the Series. The burly Robertson was surprisingly agile at first base. But those two seasons were the only big ones in a career that lasted the rest of the decade.

Robertson slammed into a railing chasing a foul ball early in the 1972 season and was never the same player after injuring his knee and back. He slumped to .172 with 12 home runs and 41 RBIs in 1972. Fans supported him admirably through the season-long struggle. His average was .239 in 1973 and his lack of production made him a bench player by 1974. The Pirates released him during spring training in 1977 and he finished with Seattle and Toronto. His career average was .242 with 115 home runs and 368 RBIs. After 1973, he never had more than 250 at-bats in a season. Robertson could have been the Pirates' biggest star. Instead, he became a bench player, and that disappointing turn places him atop this list.

79 You couldn't count how many times Jack Lambert, Willie Stargell, and Mario Lemieux had their names in headlines. But the sports scene doesn't function without hard-working people who don't always get the credit that they're due.

Here are five people who should be recognized for their contributions.

5. ART MCKENNAN

His smooth baritone boomed over the public address system at Forbes Field and was one of the few elements that made the transition to Three Rivers Stadium. Behind that big voice was a quiet, frail man who had battled polio in his youth.

Because he always comported himself with restraint when the microphone was open, most fans never knew that McKennan was an avid Pirates fan who absolutely hated to lose. His coworkers in the scoreboard room had to duck flying objects when things weren't going well for the Pirates.

McKennan, who died at age 90 in 1996, was also an amazing storehouse of baseball knowledge. When Philadelphia's Mickey Morandini pulled an unassisted triple play against the Pirates in 1992, McKennan was able to recall in precise detail two previous unassisted triple plays he had seen at Forbes Field in 1925 and 1927. His diction was perfect, his voice was mellifluous, and Art McKennan was part of the soundtrack of a lot of summers in Pittsburgh.

4. JACK BUTTON

Button was the general manager of the Penguins when the team fell into bankruptcy in the summer of 1975. He was the court-appointed receiver for the franchise. He was a hockey lifer who had no preparation for the receiver role, but he studied and worked hard to protect Pittsburgh's interest in the Penguins. The franchise was saved, and what did that earn Button? A pink slip.

The new ownership group installed Wren Blair as general manager, a move that was unfair and turned out to be destructive. Button went on to head the Central Scouting Bureau, then worked in personnel for the Washington Capitals, where he discovered Peter Bondra. Button died at age 56 in 1996 and the Jack Button Award goes to the top prospect in the Washington organization. He deserves similar recognition in Pittsburgh.

3. CHUCK KLAUSING

One of the best football coaches ever produced by western Pennsylvania, Wilmerding native Klausing did his most significant work at the high school and small college levels. His teams were 53–0–1 in six seasons at Braddock High, and he parlayed that success into assistant coaching jobs with Rutgers, Army, and West Virginia. In between the last two stops he was head coach at Indiana (Pennsylvania) and had a 47–10 record in six years, with a trip to the Boardwalk Bowl.

After West Virginia, Klausing signed on at Carnegie-Mellon and quickly established a winning program. From 1976 to 1985, he won six conference championships, earned four trips to the NCAA Division III playoffs, and had a record of 77–15–2. After one season on the staff at Pitt, Klausing closed out his career at Kiski Prep in 1993. He was 124–25–2 as a college coach, but never got the chance to take over a Division I-A program. The big schools were always interested in someone more slick. The only thing flashy about Chuck Klausing was his record.

2. JOE GORDON

After the Penguins foolishly let him go in 1969, Gordon signed on with the Steelers and stayed with the organization through 1998. His nominal title was "publicity director," but he was multitasking before anyone thought of the term. Gordon lined up sponsorships for the Steelers, negotiated the team's local broadcast contracts, booked appearances for the players, and rode herd over the media. He established a system of cooperation that depended on respect from both sides.

A former amateur athlete, Gordon had a feisty spirit. When the Steelers had a fierce rivalry with Dallas, he would exchange letters with his Cowboys counterpart and substitute a very rude two-word phrase for "Sincerely yours." Gordon also scuffled with a visiting reporter one time when he thought a line of questioning was unfair. Gordon tapped out his correspondence on a rickety typewriter well into the computer age and had a knack for dealing with visitors and phone calls simultaneously. Gordon was the one who convinced Myron Cope it was time to give up his Steelers broadcasting duties. Cope didn't question the recommendation, which speaks to the respect Gordon has earned.

1. NELLIE KING

King pitched for the Pirates in the 1950s, but he wasn't a big enough name to turn that connection into a high-profile broadcast job. So King earned his way to that spot.

He worked at local stations in Greensburg and Latrobe, calling high school games, selling commercials, and learning his craft at the grassroots level. That got him a spot in the Pirates' broadcast booth in 1967, playing third wheel to Bob Prince and Jim Woods. Prince and King were teamed from 1971 to 1975, until they were fired.

The Pirates then created a front office job for King, but his feelings were too bruised to take it. He instead signed on as Duquesne's sports information director, which wound up being one of many duties he performed for the university. He was the color analyst on basketball radio broadcasts, he lined up sponsorships, he assisted a parade of athletic directors, and he also coached the golf team. At the same time, King continued to freelance for a number of Pittsburgh radio stations on talk shows and morning sports reports. King remains one of the great storytellers in Pittsburgh. His degree of familiarity probably detracts from his importance on the local sports scene, but his varied contributions spanning six decades put him at the head of this list.

WHO WERE THE MOST OBSCURE MEMBERS OF PITTSBURGH'S CHAMPIONSHIP TEAMS?

They were part of some of the most storied teams in town, but you can't blame people for wanting to see their championship rings as proof.

They were players who didn't play that often. They were in the right place at the right time, and proudly found their place on a title-winning team in a supporting role. For every Ernie Stautner who had a distinguished career that didn't include a championship, there is a player who was treated more kindly by fate. Here are five of the most-forgotten players who were Pittsburgh champions.

JIM MANDICH, 1978 STEELERS

Mandich was a regular for the Miami Dolphins for eight seasons beginning in 1970 and was a member of the undefeated 1972 team. He wound up with the Steelers for the last year of his NFL career and suited up for ten regular-season games without catching a pass. He was on the active roster for Super Bowl XIII against Dallas.

BOB OLDIS, 1960 PIRATES

Oldis was the 32-year-old third-string catcher behind the platoon of Smoky Burgess and Hal Smith. He had scuffled to stay in the major leagues with bad teams in Washington from 1953 to1955, then spent four full seasons in the minor leagues. The Pirates picked him up in the Rule 5 draft off the New York Yankees' roster on November 11, 1959. Oldis, a good-humored man in the clubhouse, started just three games for the 1960 Pirates. He appeared in only 22 games, and didn't get into 16 of them until the 8th inning or later. Oldis batted 20 times, collecting 4 hits for a .200 average with 1 RBI. He appeared defensively for 2 innings in two World Series games.

CHARLIE SANDS, 1971 PIRATES

Sands was the third option at catcher behind Manny Sanguillen and rookie Milt May. Sands, at age 24, had been acquired from the Yankees' system in a minor league deal on October 15, 1970. He made the team as a left-handed pinch hitter. He started two games and all but three of his 28 appearances were as a pinch hitter. Sands was 5-for-25 (.200) with a home run and 5 RBIs. He got into one World Series game as a pinch hitter and struck out.

JOCK CALLANDER, 1992 PENGUINS

Callander, age 30, had appeared in 109 regular-season games but had long been written off as a nonprospect who was filling out a minor league roster. The Penguins had injuries in the playoffs and summoned him from their Cleveland farm team. Callander wound up scoring one goal and 3 points in 12 playoff games, and got his name on the Stanley Cup. Except for eight games with Tampa Bay in 1992–1993, the rest of his career was spent in the minor leagues.

DAVE MICHAYLUK, 1992 PENGUINS

Like Callander, Michayluk was toiling for the Penguins' minor league affiliate in Cleveland with little hope of getting back to the NHL. His only NHL experience had been 14 regular-season games with Philadelphia over two seasons from 1981 to 1983. Then the Penguins' depth problem cropped up in the playoffs and Michayluk was called up to join Callander, his linemate at Cleveland. He appeared in seven playoff games, scoring a goal with 1 assist. Michayluk never played in the NHL again, yet he had achieved a goal that eluded players with much longer careers. He was a Stanley Cup champion.

HITS AND MISSES

WHAT WERE THE BEST PITTSBURGH TEAMS THAT DIDN'T WIN CHAMPIONSHIPS?

81 The Pirates have won five World Series, the Steelers have five Super Bowl trophies, and the Penguins lifted the Stanley Cup twice. But, oh, those ones that got away.

Each of the three teams had seasons that ended with significant heartbreak, just short of a title that seemed to be destined.

The Pirates came up short each year from 1990 to 1992, when they took three consecutive National League East titles. Overmatched against the Reds in 1990, they had their best opportunity in 1991. They held a 3–2 lead in games over the Atlanta Braves in the 1991 playoffs and came home with two chances to close the series. But the offense fizzled, collecting 10 hits (9 singles) in the final two games, losing them 1–0 and 4–0. The Pirates hit .164 in those games.

The following year was even worse. They took a 2–0 lead into the ninth inning of the seventh game against the Atlanta Braves. Then things started to happen. Right fielder Cecil Espy misplayed a catchable ball into a double. Gold-Glove-award-winning second baseman Jose Lind made a rare error. Plate umpire Randy Marsh didn't see borderline pitches to Damon Berryhill as strikes. Pinch hitter Francisco Cabrera stroked a single to left, Barry Bonds's throw to the plate was a second late and 2 feet offline, and the Pirates lost 3–2.

But those still weren't the worst. The 1972 Pirates were even better than the team that had won the World Series the season before. The offense, first in the National League in both batting average and slugging percentage, was led by Roberto Clemente and Willie Stargell, two future Hall of Famers. The Pirates were second in earned run average. Steve Blass was 19–8 with a 2.49 ERA and Dock Ellis was 15–7, 2.70. The bullpen had the league's best right-left combination in Dave Giusti (22 saves) and Ramon Hernandez (14 saves). After a slow April, the Pirates moved into first place in mid-June and breezed to the National League East title.

They led the fifth game of the playoffs 3–2 into the bottom of the ninth against the Cincinnati Reds. Giusti, who had allowed only 3 home runs in his 74 and 2/3 innings, hung a palmball that Johnny Bench blasted for a tying homer. Two singles and a sacrifice fly later, Bob Moose uncorked a wild pitch that Manny Sanguillen didn't block, and the Pirates were losers after one of the best seasons in franchise history.

The Steelers' agonizing close call came in 1976, as they tried to become the first team to win three consecutive Super Bowls. With the team off to a 2–4 start, Terry Bradshaw was injured, which forced inexperienced Mike Kruczek to start at quarterback. That proved to be no problem, thanks to a strong running game that would result in 1,000-yard seasons for both Franco Harris and Rocky Bleier. The biggest factor, though, was a defense that made sure the offense didn't have to score many points.

The Steelers allowed just 22 points in the season's last eight games. They shut out opponents five times and held them to a single field goal in two games (the Houston Oilers scored 16 points in the other game.) At one point, the Steelers had gone five and a half games without allowing a touchdown. But Harris and Bleier were both injured in the first playoff game, a win over the Baltimore Colts. The following week the Steelers had only one available running back, Reggie Harrison, who had carried the ball just 54 times for 235 yards in the regular season. The Steelers fell to the Oakland Raiders, 24–7, in the AFC championship game.

And then there was one famous Penguins collapse, which was rooted in overconfidence. The Penguins appeared to be on their way to a third consecutive Stanley Cup in the spring of 1993. Mario Lemieux had 160 points, one of four Penguins to top 100 points. The Penguins won the Presidents Trophy by finishing first overall in the NHL, and they ended the season with a league-record 17-game winning streak.

They won their first-round series from New Jersey in five games, outscoring the Devils 26–12. The Penguins appeared to have an easy match in the second round against the New York Islanders, and apparently thought that way. Later, some players admitted they'd looked past the Islanders to the next series against Montreal. The Islanders had barely qualified for the postseason, finishing 22 points behind the Penguins. They didn't, however, play like heavy underdogs. The teams split the first four games of the playoff series. The Penguins won the fifth game but lost 7–5 on Long Island in game 6.

That set up a seventh game in Pittsburgh, which started badly for the Penguins. Left wing Kevin Stevens, who had 55 goals and 111 points in the regular season, was seriously injured when he crashed face-first to the ice after a check from Rich Pilon knocked him out. The game went to overtime. Islander David Volek, who had scored just 8 goals in the regular season, streaked down the right side and put a slap-shot past Penguin goalie Tom Barrasso at 5:16 of overtime. Game over. Entering the 2006–2007 season, that was the last playoff series the Islanders had won.

Coach Scotty Bowman left the Penguins organization after that loss, and went on to Detroit, where he won three more championships. Since that devastating loss, the Penguins have advanced beyond the second round just twice and missed the playoffs in five seasons.

WHAT WERE PITTSBURGH'S FIVE GREATEST SPORTS FASHION MISTAKES?

Clothes don't really make the man, but there's a reason players fuss with their uniforms: They want to look good out there.

Sometimes, team management makes that impossible by providing bad fashion choices. Here's a look at the five worst sartorial errors.

5. FOOL'S GOLD: PENGUINS AND PITT

Gold is an integral part of the uniform for most Pittsburgh teams, but the effect is negated by using the wrong gold. The Penguins and Pitt are both guilty. The Penguins started out with snappy uniforms that featured two shades of blue, white, and yellow.

When the Pirates and Steelers both won championships after their 1979 seasons, there was pressure for the Penguins to switch to black and gold, to match. They were in no position to resist the groundswell so they unveiled their new colors on January 30, 1980. (The Boston Bruins' protested unsuccessfully to the NHL on copycat grounds.) The Penguin black and gold was fine up until the 1999–2000 season, when the Penguins switched the bright gold to a more muted shade called "Las Vegas Gold." As a result, their color scheme now more closely resembles the New Orleans Saints than the Steelers. If they want to jump off the black and gold bandwagon, they should go back to two shades of blue.

Meanwhile, one of the many tweaks to the Pitt uniform has been a similar shift to a lesser gold. A lot of fans don't like it, but the administration is holding firm and won't bring back the brighter gold, which is just a shade or two away from the paint used on school buses.

4. HELMETS IN THE FIELD: PIRATES

The Pirates introduced the batting helmet in 1953. Good idea. Batters needed the protection, and Pirates general manager Branch Rickey owned stock in the company that made the fiberglass headgear. But Rickey had such enthusiasm for the innovation that he insisted the players wear them in the field as well. Baseball cards of that era show pitchers completing their windup with a helmet on their heads. The heckling from other dugouts was relentless and the players were allowed to ditch the helmets in the field within a few weeks.

The helmet became entrenched for batters, though. In later years, a few players would voluntarily wear a helmet while playing defense. Long-time first baseman John Olerud was required to wear a helmet at all times after undergoing brain surgery early in his career.

3. THROWBACKS: STEELERS

The Steelers celebrated the NFL's 75th anniversary in 1994 by wearing throwback uniforms for selected games. The version they chose was a design from the early days of the franchise, which was founded in 1933. The players wore jerseys with loud stripes and the city of Pittsburgh's crest on the front. Steelers chairman Dan Rooney apparently had a fondness for the style. His was a minority opinion, though. The NFL sells tons of merchandise to fans, but it doesn't offer a version of these jerseys. They read the market apathy correctly.

2. GEOMETRIC SHOULDERS: STEELERS

The 1967 uniform was close to the current version with one huge exception: The shoulders featured a gold triangular pattern that came to a point at the player's sternum. The idea was to tie into Pittsburgh's Golden Triangle, the downtown point where the Allegheny and Monongahela rivers meet to form the Ohio River. The concept may have been noble, but the jerseys embarrassed the players. They were mothballed after Chuck Noll came to town and started upgrading all aspects of the Steelers' operation.

1. MIX AND MATCH: PIRATES

The team that pioneered beltless, buttonless doubleknits for the 1970 debut of Three Rivers Stadium realized its once innovative look had gone stale by the middle of the decade. So they made baseball fashion history again by abandoning the traditional concept of home and road uniforms.

They came up with three basic designs—all black, all gold, and white striped—that could also be mixed and matched. That created nine basic possibilities. The variations grew with the accessories—stirrup socks, undershirts, and caps all came in black or gold. The problem? The gold they used was a shade of a canary yellow that made sunglasses a necessity. Plus, the Pirates looked like the Steelers when they wore black jerseys and gold pants. The stripes were fine as a solid uniform, but a disaster when they were mixed with either the black or gold.

The uniform of the day was hung in each locker by equipment manager John Hallahan and his staff. He carried out the orders that came from the front office. The daily uniform choice was made by June Schaut, the executive assistant to team vice president Joe O'Toole. She would choose the combination, then presumably sit back and snicker at the mess she created. Someone overdid a good idea and the Pirates' garish combinations are an easy choice as the number-one fashion mistake.

The variations disappeared over the years, with the stripes going first. By the mid-1980s, the Pirates were back to a more traditional look, although the horizontally striped black caps lingered for a few years. When pitcher Brian Fisher got the word that the Yankees had traded him to the Pirates after the 1986 season, he said his first reaction was, "Oh no, they wear those round hats." Fortunately for Fisher, the Pirates ditched the odd caps before he arrived.

Just for the record, here's what the Pirates were wearing when they won the 1979 World Series in Baltimore: gold jersey, black pants, black sleeves, gold stirrups, and black caps.

WHO WERE THE BIGGEST TORTURED SOULS OF PITTSBURGH SPORTS?

It takes all kinds of personalities to make up a team. Sometimes they're odd or unusual in a fun way, like the free-spirited Bryan Watson, who once commandeered a hotel courtesy van on a trip with the Penguins. Others distinguish themselves with demons they bring to the world of fun and games.

Here's a look at five Pittsburgh players who were memorable for that reason.

BRIAN "SPINNER" SPENCER. PENGUINS

Spencer was a fan favorite in his short time with the Penguins (86 games from 1977 to 1978), a high-energy player with long curly hair who had far more hustle than talent. He was willing to play a physical game and he always seemed to enjoy himself on the ice. He had the team's most unique vehicle, a custom-made monstrosity he called "The Hulk." Spencer had stripped down a 2 1/2-ton Army truck, installed a diesel engine, and then placed the shell of a 1972 Dodge van on the chassis. He'd offer free tours to any fans who wanted to explore his creation. But Spencer's fun-loving exterior covered up a past tragedy.

On December 12, 1970, he was scheduled to be the intermission guest on Hockey Night in Canada's coverage of the Toronto Maple Leafs game. He called his parents with the news. But Spencer's family lived in western Canada, where the local affiliate was providing coverage of the Vancouver Canucks rather than the Leafs. Spencer's father Roy stormed the television station with a gun and demanded they switch to the Toronto game. A standoff followed and Roy Spencer was shot to death by police.

The tragedy haunted Spencer throughout his life, although his hockey career provided a welcome distraction. When Spencer lost the structure that came with playing hockey, his life took a series of wrong turns. Spencer wound up in Florida. In 1987, he was charged with murder and faced the death penalty. Cleared of those charges, he met a violent end on June 2, 1988. He was shot and killed while he was allegedly trying to buy crack cocaine. A book and TV movie were later devoted to Spencer's star-crossed life.

ERNIE HOLMES, STEELERS

Holmes played for the Steelers from 1972 to 1977. This 325-pound-plus mountain of a defensive tackle was one member of the defensive front four that wound up on the cover of *Time* magazine in the 1970s. In 1974, he had his hair sculpted into an arrow to "point the way to the Super Bowl." He was also involved in his share of controversy.

In the spring of 1973, he was driving back to Pittsburgh in the hope of making some extra money playing on the Steelers' off-season basketball team. Holmes was despondent over the breakup of his marriage and concerned that he wouldn't be able to spend time with his two children. As the stress mounted, he became convinced trucks were trying to force him off the Ohio Turnpike. Holmes grabbed a gun and fired at the trucks. When a police helicopter pursued his car, he fired at the helicopter, too.

Holmes pleaded guilty to charges of assault with a deadly weapon, which got him five years of probation and two months in a psychiatric hospital. Although Joe Greene tried to distance himself from the brutality of the football field, Holmes seemed to embrace it. Even after his arrest, he kept a piranha in his apartment and fed it a goldfish each day. He told *Time*'s interviewer, "I don't know what my life is, except there's something pounding in the back of my head."

STEVE DURBANO, PENGUINS

Fans called him "Demolition Durby," and Durbano relished his image as one of the toughest players in hockey. Before rules cracked down on bench-clearing brawls, Durbano was a leading proponent of mayhem on the ice. *The Hockey News* called him "Hockey's baddest man" in a 1988 poll, well after Durbano's career had ended. Some players grudgingly accept a role as an enforcer; Durbano loved it, along with the notoriety the job brought.

His life after hockey was tumultuous. In 1983 he was implicated in a scheme to import cocaine and spent seven years in prison. He later had other brushes with the law—Durbano was picked up for shoplifting clothes, then was arrested when he tried to recruit an undercover police officer to work for an escort service. "He was a good-hearted guy who made bad decisions," said former NHL player Dale Tallon, a childhood friend of Durbano's. Durbano died of liver cancer in 2002, just short of his 52nd birthday.

JOHN BRISKER, CONDORS

This 6-foot, 5-inch Detroit native was the biggest star of the Condors' ill-fated three-year run in Pittsburgh. Brisker was a talented player. In his three seasons, he averaged 21,

29.3, and 28.9 points per game. But his inability to control his anger caused problems. His temper made him notorious around the ABA, and made Condors teammates reluctant to practice against him.

He was ejected from a game against Denver for elbowing Art Becker. A few moments later, he rushed back onto the court to slug Becker, who was standing at the free throw line. His rage extended to his off-field life: Brisker attended one of the Pirates' games in the 1971 World Series and wound up being handcuffed by police after a confrontation with a cab driver.

When the Condors folded in 1972, Brisker went to the NBA and played for Seattle. In 1978 he boarded a plane for Africa and was never heard from again. No one is quite sure why Brisker went there. The most popular theory was he had gone to work for Ugandan dictator Idi Amin. It was presumed he was killed in an uprising. Brisker was declared legally dead in 1985 at age 38.

ROD SCURRY, PIRATES

Scurry had a devastating curveball, which led the Pirates to draft the left-hander in the first round in 1974. He reached the major leagues in 1980. Then Scurry started using cocaine, and admitted his use was out of control in 1984. He headed to rehab. The press conference upon his return was chilling. The usually scraggly Scurry had short hair and was clean shaven. He looked like a different person and struggled with his emotions as he described how cocaine came to rule his life. Manager Chuck Tanner offered support. Teammate Bill Madlock was on hand for the same purpose, but his occasional vague comments made it clear he had no real relationship with Scurry, who was distant from most teammates.

A year later Scurry was in trouble again for failing to follow his aftercare program. The Pirates sold him to the New York Yankees, and Scurry's name would occasionally resurface in stories about drug problems. He testified in the 1985 baseball drug trials that were held in Pittsburgh. Scurry also spent some time with the Seattle Mariners, pitching his last major league game for them on September 30, 1988.

In the fall of 1992, Scurry was involved in an incident in Nevada in which he was acting erratically, claiming snakes were trying to attack him. Sheriff's deputies removed him and he stopped breathing while in their custody. He became unconscious on his way to an intensive care unit and died one week later on November 5. Scurry's son, also named Rod, is a 6-foot, 7-inch right-handed pitcher at the University of Nevada. He was drafted by the Colorado Rockies in 2005.

WHO ARE FIVE FAMOUS PLAYERS NO ONE REMEMBERS WEARING A PITTSBURGH UNIFORM?

84 Remember when Franco Harris finished his career with the Seattle Seahawks? Not many people do. A contract dispute ended Harris's career with the Steelers and he spent one season with the Seahawks.

After nearly two decades with the Pirates, Elroy Face wound up his career with short stays with the Detroit Tigers and Montreal Expos. Willie Stargell ended up coaching for the Atlanta Braves after spending his entire playing career with the Pirates.

It works the other way, too. Players closely associated with other teams sometimes wind up with one of the Pittsburgh teams. Here's a look at a few players who did just that.

BO BELINSKY

He was the most famous sports playboy before Joe Namath, a streetwise New Jersey pool hustler who became one of the first stars of the expansion Los Angeles Angels in the early 1960s. Belinsky had a memorable name and a penchant for dating actresses such as Mamie Van Doren and Tina Louise. He pitched a no-hitter against Baltimore on May 5, 1962, and helped draw some publicity away from the better-known Dodgers. Belinsky started the 1962 season 5–0 and improved to 7–1, but finished 10–11, which more or less typified his disappointing career. He pitched in relief for the Pirates in 1969, his next-to-last major league stop. Belinsky was 0–3 in eight games with a 4.58 earned run average.

MICKEY VERNON

A friend of Pirates manager Danny Murtaugh, Vernon joined the Pirates' coaching staff in 1960. He was activated for the last month of the season at age 42 and ended his 20-year career with 1 hit in 8 at-bats. That limited action in 1960 allowed Vernon to become a four-decade player. The last nine of Vernon's 2,409 career games were with the Pirates. He was best known for his long career in the American League, which included batting championships in 1946 and 1953.

MARION MOTLEY

The star fullback of the Cleveland Browns came out of retirement in 1955 and played for the Steelers. He appeared in just 7 games, carrying the ball two times for 8 yards. Motley led the running game for coach Paul Brown when his Cleveland teams won four straight All American Football Conference titles from 1946 to 1949. The injury issues that forced Motley to retire after the 1953 season returned, and he cut short his only season with the Steelers. Motley was elected to the Pro Football Hall of Fame in 1968.

TIM HORTON

After 18 seasons with the Toronto Maple Leafs and one with the New York Rangers, Horton landed with the Penguins from 1971 to 1972. The connection was coach Red Kelly, who had been a Toronto teammate of Horton's. It was the one and only season Horton spent with the Penguins, but he had played in Pittsburgh before. He spent three seasons (1949 to 1952) with the minor league Pittsburgh Hornets before he got to the NHL. Horton was killed in a 1974 highway accident, but his name lives on through the coffee and doughnut franchises that bear his name throughout Canada.

DEREK SANDERSON

He was one of sports' most notorious bachelors in the late 1960s and early 1970s. Sanderson, nicknamed "The Turk," drove a Rolls Royce, told an interviewer his pregame routine was "a steak and a blonde," and was named one of the sexiest men in America by *Cosmopolitan* magazine. By the time he reached Pittsburgh, he was at the end of the line in a career that had been wrecked by substance abuse and poor financial decisions.

The Penguins signed him late in the 1977–1978 season, hoping he could help on the ice and at the box office. They were too late on both counts. Sanderson was over the hill at age 32 and could barely catch his breath after skating a shift. He appeared in 13 games and scored the last 3 goals of his professional career with the Penguins. Sanderson turned his life around after hockey, working first as a broadcaster and later with a firm that advises athletes on investing their earnings. He does extensive charity work in the Boston area, where no one has memories of him gasping for air on the bench of a lousy 1978 Penguins team.

WHO WERE PITTSBURGH'S GREATEST FLASHES IN THE PAN?

You may think we've covered this ground before with question 78, "Which players had careers that made you say, 'Is that all there is?'"

But there's a distinct difference. The earlier argument tackled players who established themselves and developed expectations that they didn't live up to. Flashes in the pan, on the other hand, are players who come out of nowhere, are impressive for a short period of time, and then disappear again.

Here's a look at five players who offered a lot of promise for a while, but were unable to sustain their success.

5. JIM NELSON, PIRATES

Nelson is the answer to the trivia question: Who was the winning pitcher in the last game at Forbes Field? The 22-year-old right-hander reached the major leagues for the first time just a month before the Pirates closed the old ballpark with a doubleheader sweep of the Chicago Cubs on June 28, 1970. Nelson was 4–2 with a 3.42 earned run average for the Pirates in 1970 and 2–2 with a 2.34 ERA in 1971. But rotator cuff problems followed and his major league career was confined to 32 games over those two seasons. He pitched the 16th and 17th innings of a home victory over San Diego on July 15, 1971, in his last major league game.

4. DINO RESTELLI, PIRATES

Talk about instant excitement. The Pirates bought Restelli, a 24-year-old outfielder from a minor league San Francisco Seals in the Pacific Coast League in 1949, and he promptly hit 8 home runs in his first 10 major league games. But it didn't take long for pitchers to adjust, and Restelli wound up with just 2 more home runs in his next 72 major league games. He spent 1950 back in the minor leagues and his last major league experience was a 21-game stay in 1951 that produced a .184 average and 1 home run in 38 at-bats. Restelli later became a policeman in San Francisco.

3. WARREN MORRIS, PIRATES

The Pirates traded enigmatic pitcher Esteban Loaiza to Texas to get Morris in 1998 and the deal looked like a steal a year later. Morris broke into the 1999 starting lineup as a rookie, batting .288 with fifteen home runs and 73 runs batted in 147 games. He finished a strong third behind Scott Williamson and Preston Wilson in the National League's Rookie of the Year voting.

The next season Morris was a different player, hitting only 3 home runs with 43 RBIs in 528 at-bats. He was released during spring training of 2002 and wound up playing with six organizations over three years before he retired. Morris hit 15 home runs in his first 511 major league at-bats; in 984 subsequent at-bats, he hit just 11.

2. TOMMY MADDOX, STEELERS

Maddox signed with the Steelers as a free agent in 2001, fresh from reviving his career in the short-lived XFL, where

263

he was the league's Most Valuable Player. Maddox came out of UCLA after his sophomore season and was drafted on the first round by the Denver Broncos in 1992. He bounced around to two other NFL teams and tried Arena Football before the start-up XFL lured him out of retirement (Maddox had been working in the insurance business).

By the fourth game of 2002 he had replaced Kordell Stewart as the Steelers starter and took the team to a 10–5–1 record and the playoffs. Maddox helped the Steelers rally from a 17-point 3rd-quarter deficit against the Cleveland Browns in the playoffs. He was the NFL's Comeback Player of the Year. The following season, the Steelers slumped to 6–10. Then Maddox was injured in the second game of 2004 and replaced by rookie Ben Roethlisberger. A season later, Maddox played poorly when filling in for the injured Roethlisberger and fell behind Charlie Batch on the depth chart. He discovered how tough Pittsburgh can be on quarterbacks who don't win. Maddox retired after the 2005 season, unable to duplicate the success he'd enjoyed in 2002.

1. WARREN YOUNG, PENGUINS

Young was a 6-foot, 3-inch, 200-pound winger who made the team in 1984 by his willingness to fight. The Penguins were looking for players to help protect rookie Mario Lemieux, and Young fit the bill. In parts of three previous NHL seasons with Minnesota and Pittsburgh, Young had managed 2 goals and 10 points in 20 games. At age 28, he didn't figure to improve.

But when Lemieux made his debut at home on October 17, 1984, Young scored a couple of goals. Within a few weeks, Lemieux requested that Young be one of his line-mates. Young scored 40 goals and 72 points. His timing was perfect. He hit the free agent market that off-season and got a lucrative free agent contract from the Detroit Red Wings. The Red Wings ate most of that contract, releasing Young after he had a disappointing season with 22 goals and 46 points. He wound up back with the Penguins in a lesser role and split time between the NHL and minor leagues. In his one season as Lemieux's left wing, Young had 40 goals in 80 games. He scored 32 goals in his other 156 NHL games. Of all the players who came and went quickly, Young's star set the standards for being both bright and brief.

WHAT WAS PITTSBURGH'S WORST SPORTS HIRE?

86 The clarity of hindsight is amazing. Look over this list and you wonder how certain people were hired for certain jobs. But apparently they all made some sense at the time. They stack up as horrendous decisions now. Here are the five worst hires.

5. EDDIE OLCZYK, PENGUINS COACH, 2003–2004 SEASON

The Penguins weren't going to bring back interim coach Rick Kehoe, and Olczyk, who was the Penguins' TV analyst, was interested in the job. That was fine by general manager Craig Patrick, who hired Olczyk without interviewing anyone else. It must have been an impressive interview, because Olczyk had no previous coaching experience.

The Penguins knew they had a bad team as they awaited the inevitable labor stoppage that would change the NHL's financial structure. Patrick called it "survival mode." So Olczyk wasn't a risky hire, and the Penguins were as bad as expected (23–47–8). But after the one-year layoff brought on by the lockout, Patrick brought Olczyk back to lead a team that had spent money on free agents, drafted Sidney Crosby, and had playoff expectations. Instead the season was a disaster. The Penguins were 8–17–6 in mid-December when Olczyk was fired and replaced by Michel Therrien. The Penguins were back in the playoffs in Therrien's first full season.

4. BILL AUSTIN, HEAD COACH, STEELERS, 1966

Austin had the distinction of being the last head coach hired by Steelers founder Art Rooney Sr. As usual, Rooney leaned heavily on the recommendations of his NFL cronies when he needed a coach. Austin came with some enthusiastic endorsements, including Vince Lombardi's. Austin had served as Lombardi's top aide in Green Bay.

But the Steelers didn't have enough talent, and Austin didn't have the credentials to pull off Lombardi's demanding style. The Steelers were 5–8–1 in Austin's first year, and things went downhill from there. They were 4–9–1 in 1967 and then fell to 2–11–1 in his final season. After that season, Dan Rooney took responsibility for hiring the new head coach and brought in Chuck Noll.

3. A SUCCESSION OF STEELERS OFFENSIVE COORDINATORS

The list includes Joe Walton (1990–1991), Ray Sherman (1998), and Kevin Gilbride (1999–2000). Walton came in with solid credentials after serving as the Washington Redskins' offensive coordinator and the head coach of the New York Jets. But Steelers players complained that Walton's offense was too complicated, and quarterback Bubby Brister was the most vocal critic. Sherman was brought in with the hope that he could help quarterback Kordell Stewart develop, but the two never had any chemistry. Sherman resigned after one rocky season. Things went from bad to worse with Gilbride, who tried to rein in Stewart's tendency to improvise and take off running. Stewart once scored a touchdown and was immediately castigated by Gilbride for failing to follow instructions.

2. PIERRE CREAMER, PENGUINS COACH, 1987

Bob Berry was dismissed after three nonplayoff seasons, and general manager Eddie Johnston hired Creamer, the 43-year-old coach of the Montreal Canadiens' top farm team. Creamer was also the brother-in-law of New York Islanders star Mike Bossy.

Creamer knew hockey, but couldn't communicate that knowledge to most of his players. He struggled with English, and the players soon stopped paying attention. The Penguins had enough talent to make the playoffs but Creamer couldn't corral them. Late in the season, the Penguins needed to win a game at Washington to keep their faint playoff hopes alive. Players waited for Creamer to pull his goalie in a tie game. Creamer didn't realize a tie would do the Penguins no good. Players were frantically try to explain the situation to their clueless coach. Finally the players summoned the goalie to the bench and the Penguins won the game. Less than two weeks after the season, Tony Esposito was hired to replace Johnston as general manager. Creamer was fired that summer and his season in the NHL wound up being the end of his coaching career.

1. MILO HAMILTON, PIRATES BROADCASTER, 1976

Bob Prince's firing after 28 years was controversial and guaranteed that anyone stepping into the broadcast booth to replace him would face challenging circumstances. Ray Scott, who had worked in Pittsburgh before becoming CBS-TV's lead NFL announcer, said he wouldn't be interested in trying to follow Prince. Fans were angry over Prince's dismissal and were ready to take it out on his successor. Under those circumstances, the Pirates needed a secure individual who paid little attention to outside influences. Instead, they approved the hiring of Hamilton, who had been cut loose by the Atlanta Braves after the 1975 season.

Hamilton seemingly saw and heard every slight directed at him, and often felt the need to respond. When a *Pittsburgh Post-Gazette* football writer included a flippant reference to someone being nearly as unpopular as Milo

Hamilton, Hamilton sought out the writer and wanted to physically confront him in the press box.

Hamilton's dry-as-dust, factoid-laden style was in direct contrast to Prince's folksy storytelling, and that was also jarring for the audience. Prince was the Voice of the Pirates; Hamilton was another generic announcer passing through town because that's where a job opportunity existed.

It was a bad match and it lasted four years until Hamilton jumped at a chance to move into the Chicago Cubs' booth. Instead of replacing a legend there, he was supplanted by one. Hamilton was bumped to second-banana status when Harry Caray was hired by the Cubs. Hamilton spent the rest of his career in Houston, where no legends diminished him by comparison.

THEY'RE 'BURGH THINGS

WHAT WAS PITTSBURGH'S BEST NOW-DEFUNCT FRANCHISE?

87 The Pirates were established in 1887, the Steelers are the NFL's fifth-oldest franchise, and the Penguins were born in the NHL's first great expansion of 1967. In that context of stability, it's easy to lose track of franchises that have come and gone over the years.

The city has had at least four pro basketball franchises, one upstart pro football team, Arena football, a couple of tries at indoor soccer, even more attempts at traditional soccer, World Team Tennis, indoor lacrosse, and roller hockey. Some barely made a ripple, and some drew enough fans and had enough success to create some fond memories. For what it's worth, the first Arena Football championship, the Arena Bowl, was played in Pittsburgh, but the hometown Gladiators lost.

There was a soccer team called the Phantoms that played its games at Forbes Field in its one and only season, 1967. That was the first year soccer was going to be the next big thing, and CBS even televised games. The Phantoms were a dismal flop, with an average attendance of 3,122, which was second-worst in the National Professional Soccer League. The Pirates complained that the soccer games chewed up the outfield grass, which meant the Phantoms players actually helped two teams fail on their way to a record of 10–14–7. About the only thing anyone remembers concerning the appropriately named Phantoms is that they had a player named Co Prins, so it's sad to report that he died while playing soccer on September 28, 1987, just 20 years after the Phantoms vanished.

The Phantoms' name was resurrected for a roller hockey team that actually had NHL Hall of Famer Bryan Trottier on its roster. That wasn't enough to make people want summer hockey, though, and the team quickly died. A little more long-lasting was the attempt at Arena Football, which stuck around for four years, 1987 through 1990, until the Gladiators moved to Florida and became the Tampa Bay Storm.

Those teams all had their followings, but let's look at the five whose parting created the most sorrow.

5. PITTSBURGH PIRANHAS, CONTINENTAL BASKETBALL ASSOCIATION, 1994–1995

The operators of the franchise had some circumstances in their favor. They started in the fall of 1994, months after Major League Baseball had been shut down by a strike and in the midst of the National Hockey League's lockout. Sure, there was the formidable shadow of the Steelers, but there had to be some extra dollars out there and fans anxious for some games. The Piranhas couldn't cash in, however, even though the CBA was a pretty good caliber of basketball. Rather than selling that point, the franchise went for some cartoon TV commercials with a killer fish. They must have looked great at the agency, but they didn't do anything to deliver the message. The Piranhas never caught on, and were gone after one season.

4. PITTSBURGH SPIRIT, INDOOR SOCCER, 1978–1979 AND 1982–1986

Yes, it was wimpy and gimmicky, but the Spirit plugged into the soccer-playing masses in middle schools and drew respectable crowds. After a rough start (they suspended operations after one season), the team was back and carved out a place in the local sports scene. Stan Terlecki was the franchise's biggest star, and some of the games were even on TV. The Spirit was relentless in getting players out in the community for instructional clinics and other appearances. It often seemed as if it was easier to get a Spirit autograph than it was to get your groceries bagged at Giant Eagle on a lot of Saturdays. Eventually enthusiasm for the team died down, however, and the Spirit faded away.

3. PITTSBURGH MAULERS, UNITED STATES FOOTBALL LEAGUE, 1984

Great idea, lousy execution. Edward DeBartolo Sr. bankrolled the spring football franchise, a solid bet in football-mad Pittsburgh. But his problems developed when he put the wrong people in charge. Paul Martha, a former Pitt All-American and former Steelers' number-one draft pick, was overmatched as the franchise's CEO. George Heddleston, a public relations man for DeBartolo's San Francisco 49ers, was hired as general manager and proved to be equally inept.

The Maulers went 3–15, which led to their most famous trivia note: They had as many victories as they did head coaches. Original coach Joe Pendry was summoned to a meeting with DeBartolo in Youngstown, Ohio, when the team was 2–8. Pendry was certain he was going to be fired, so he didn't go. DeBartolo maintained he had no intention of firing Pendry, but had no choice after he skipped the meeting. Ellis Rainsberger finished the season, and Hank Bullough was named the coach for the 1985 season that never came.

It had looked so promising before the 1984 season, when the Maulers outbid the Houston Oilers for Heisman-Trophy-winner Mike Rozier. The Nebraska running back was a disappointment, though, gaining just 792 yards. The disappointment carried over to the defense, which yielded a league-high 492 points that year, certainly distinguishing them from the Steelers. (By the way, the Steelers were not happy that the Maulers were allowed to play in Three Rivers Stadium. In fact, they didn't like anything about the USFL. When the Steelers' longtime statistics crew agreed to work for the Maulers, they were shocked when the NFL season came around and they discovered the Steelers had replaced all of them.)

The crowds came in the beginning—a lot of people showed up for an early season game against Birmingham just to throw snowballs at former Steelers quarterback Cliff Stoudt—but attendance faded as the lost season dragged on through June. Despite that, the Maulers wound up with a respectable average of 22,858, with many fans sporting the distinctive purple and orange colors.

When USFL leadership insisted on shifting to a fall schedule in an attempt to force a merger with the NFL, DeBartolo gave up. The Maulers merged with the Philadelphia franchise. They did have a going-out-of-business sale, where fans could buy uniforms and other equipment.

2. PITTSBURGH PIPERS, AMERICAN BASKETBALL ASSOCIATION, 1967–1968

Connie Hawkins made this franchise. The Brooklyn-born Hawkins was a playground legend who had first dunked a basketball at age 11. He should have been starring in the NBA, but the league had banned him because his name had surfaced during an investigation of a point-shaving scandal at the University of Iowa. The ABA welcomed Hawkins, and Pittsburgh got him, giving the Pipers a star player and an identity. The 6-foot, 8-inch, 215-pound Hawkins was the ABA's first Most Valuable Player as he led the team to a 54–24 record in the regular season. Vince Cazzetta coached the Pipers, whose starting lineup also featured Tom Washington, Art Heyman, Chico Vaughn, and Charlie Williams. The Pipers won the championship and Hawkins was also the postseason MVP. That season should have been a launching pad for big things. Instead, the Pipers abandoned Pittsburgh. While the team was winning the ABA title, a deal had already been made to move the franchise to Minneapolis. The Pipers came back to Pittsburgh a year later, but Hawkins was gone to the NBA after he successfully sued to gain admission to the league. Pro basketball in Pittsburgh was never the same, in part because of the standard Hawkins and the Pipers established in their inaugural season.

1. PITTSBURGH TRIANGLES, WORLD TEAM TENNIS, 1974–1976

Tennis was the trendy sport in the early 1970s, and Pittsburgher Chuck Reichblum first hatched the idea of a team tennis league. Pittsburgh got one of the 16 franchises and two of the biggest names—player/coach Ken Rosewall and Evonne Goolagong. The Triangles—named for the point at the confluence of the city's three rivers—also had a colorful young upstart in Vitas Gerulaitis. One of the biggest stars would become owner Frank Fuhrer, a heretofore anonymous insurance millionaire who had a streak of Steinbrenner. When he called Goolagong in for a pep talk that left her in tears, sportscaster Myron Cope dubbed the demanding owner "Der Fuhrer." Fuhrer didn't mind the attention.

The Civic Arena was packed for the opening match against Billie Jean King's Philadelphia Freedom. Fans were encouraged to abandon the restraint that traditionally ruled tennis crowds. King loved it. When she smilingly repeated an especially vile obscenity that had been directed at her by a fan, the very proper Rosewall mumbled, "Lot of good that did for tennis" and stomped out of the post-match press conference.

Weather permitting, the arena's retractable roof was opened and fans could enjoy indoor tennis with a breeze and sunset. For two years, the team drew the most attractive crowds of tanned suburbanites in pastel tennis clothing.

The team was 30–14 in its first year, but lost in the playoffs. Vic Edwards replaced Rosewall as coach in the second season and the Triangles beat San Francisco to claim the league's Bancroft Cup. With Rosewall gone, the outgoing Gerulaitis became the team's male star. His fan club was named the G-Men, and even Fuhrer was photographed wearing a club t-shirt. During one match Gerulaitis invited the entire crowd to his 20th birthday party by having public address announcer Jack Henry give the location, a nearby hotel.

The Triangles' party ended the next season. The team fell apart, Fuhrer grew impatient, crowds dwindled, and publicity man Dan McGibbeny, who had never played tennis, somehow wound up as coach (after succeeding the team doctor in that role). The Triangles played their last match against the New York Sets on August 19, 1976, in front of 2,608 fans, an ignominious end to what had been a wonderfully unconventional addition to the usually blue-collar local sports scene.. In a touch of class, Fuhrer threw a luncheon at the upscale Duquesne Club to announce the demise of the Triangles. It was a fitting sendoff for the city's best short-term franchise.

WHO ARE PITTSBURGH'S MOST HATED OPPONENTS?

There's nothing quite like a beer-tossing, fist-flying rivalry to spice up a big game. But rivalries come and go, depending on how competitive both teams are and what's at stake when they play. Take the Dallas Cowboys and the Steelers, who met three times in the Super Bowl, with Pittsburgh winning twice. It was the ultimate clash of cultures, the glitzy Cowboys with their computer scouting and cheerleaders against the working-class Steelers. It could have been huge if they had played more regularly. But alas, other fires burned brighter.

What about the Penguins/Sabres? The Penguins used to play a lot of Saturday night home games, and several of them would invariably be against the Buffalo Sabres. That timing gave Sabres fans a chance to load up a few buses and come down to Pittsburgh for the game. Since the fans weren't doing the driving, they could load up on beer along the way and lose their remaining inhibitions by the time they reached Pittsburgh. That made for some interesting scenes in the stands: Fans would be pummeling each other, while the players stood by smiling, watching the lunacy of someone else fighting for once. Interesting, but not the best battles around.

The Pirates had some heat with the New York Mets in the late 1980s. It started after the upstart Pirates won a game and Dwight Gooden said they looked "like a bunch of Little Leaguers" jumping around in celebration. Pirates management fanned the flames with a series of tasteless TV commercials offering "Another reason to hate New York." Another good try, but this one doesn't make our list either.

And here's our list—take a look at the five best rivalries that have burned with varying degrees of intensity over the years.

5. PENGUINS VS. WASHINGTON CAPITALS

Geography made this one convenient, along with the fact that the Penguins and Capitals had five Stanley Cup playoff series in six years from 1991 to 1996, then two more in 2000–2001. The Penguins won all but one of those series. More spice was added when the Penguins traded Jaromir Jagr to the Capitals in 2001. Penguins fans were so diligent about making the turnpike trip to Washington that the Capitals installed systems to keep callers with western Pennsylvania area codes from buying tickets. Too one-sided to rage out of control, this one still stirred emotions.

4. PIRATES VS. PHILADELPHIA PHILLIES

This one was ultra-hot in the 1970s when the Pirates and Phillies were battling for the National League East title. There was only one season (1973) in which either the Pirates or Phillies didn't finish in first place. Things got crazy with beanballs in the late 1970s, which led to laid-back Mike Schmidt charging the mound to get at Pirates pitcher Bruce Kison. The Phillies were easy to dislike, with lumbering Greg Luzinski and sneering Larry Bowa in their lineup. They were good enough to respect, too. From the mid-1970s to early 1980s, this was as good as any rivalry in baseball.

3. STEELERS VS. HOUSTON OILERS

This is a perfect example of circumstances creating enemies. Who could have imagined that the Oilers, an old-school American Football League team, would wind up having major hostility with the Steelers, one of the NFL's most traditional franchises? But after the AFL-NFL merger, the teams landed in the same division and they competed for the top spot. There were two Oilers-Steelers AFC championship games at Three Rivers Stadium, both won by the Steelers. One factor that prevented true hate was the presence of Bum Phillips, a genuinely nice guy and the Oilers' country bumpkin coach, who wore a ten-gallon hat on the sidelines. The Oilers were easier to dislike later when they were coached by wisecracking Jerry Glanville. Remember the infamous 1987 postgame handshake, in which Chuck Noll refused to release his grip on Glanville, all the while lecturing him about the consequences of dirty play?

2. CLEVELAND BROWNS VS. THE STEELERS

When the Steelers agreed to transfer to the American Conference as part of the 1970 AFL-NFL merger, one of their terms was insisting the Browns went with them. They weren't willing to lose that history, even though it was stacked in the Browns' favor. Excellent idea. Even if neither team is in contention, there's always a contentious relationship between the two cities. The secret reason for the hostility is that Pittsburgh and Cleveland are so similar. They both have lousy weather, they've both been victimized by the loss of heavy industry, and they both regard football as something just short of religion. When the Steelers had a fight with an opponent during warm-ups a few years ago, it's no coincidence that Cleveland was the other team. There was a bit of a void when Art Modell sold out Cleveland and moved the team to Baltimore in 1996, but when the NFL placed an expansion franchise in Cleveland in 1999, Steelers fans were fulfilled again by the prospect of hating those orange helmets twice a year.

1. OAKLAND RAIDERS VS. STEELERS

It doesn't mean much these days because the Raiders are down, plus they're found infrequently on the Steelers schedule. But in the 1970s, this was as mean and nasty as it could get. The Raiders have always taken their cue from owner Al Davis, whose cold-blooded business sense led him to take his franchise to Los Angeles for 13 years, then move it back to Oakland when that city made a better offer.

Between the two clubs, there have been many charges of dirty tricks on both sides. The Steelers accused the Raiders' linemen of slathering their jerseys with Vaseline so they could slip away from blocks. The Raiders maintain the Steelers allowed the edges of the field to freeze before the 1976 AFC championship game. Icy sidelines would affect the Raiders' passing game without having an impact on the Steelers' run-oriented offense. After the same game, Davis complained bitterly that the clock operator had allowed seconds to lapse, giving the Steelers an advantage.

It all started in 1972, when Raiders player Bob Moore was clubbed outside the team's Pittsburgh hotel the night before a playoff game. That game featured the most famous play in Steelers history, Franco Harris's touchdown on a deflected pass that became known as the "Immaculate Reception." To this day, the Raiders insist the play was illegal.

Nothing validates a rivalry like a grudge that's held for 35 years.

WHICH PITTSBURGH SPORTS FIGURE DESERVES THE NEXT STATUE?

Once there was just one sports statue in Pittsburgh. Honus Wagner, the Pirates' turn-of-the-century star, was honored with a life-sized statue that was dedicated in 1955. It sat outside of Forbes Field until it was moved to Gate C at Three Rivers Stadium in 1971.

Wagner stood alone until 1994, when the Pirates commissioned a statue of Roberto Clemente to be dedicated during the All-Star week festivities. The bronze sculpture of Clemente following through on his swing was placed at Gate A at Three Rivers. And there's one more: The Pirates ordered a statue of Willie Stargell to coincide with the April 2001 opening of PNC Park. The statue was unveiled on April 7, two days before Stargell died. Today, Stargell's statue is at the left-field entrance of PNC Park, just down Federal Street from the Clemente statue. Wagner's statue is located at the home plate entrance of PNC Park.

But football has a monument as well. The Steelers honored franchise founder Art Rooney with a statue that was dedicated on November 4, 1990, at Gate B of Three Rivers Stadium. The Rooney statue is now on the lawn outside the open end of Heinz Field, near its old Three Rivers Stadium location.

So who's next? The Penguins' new arena will undoubtedly include a monument to Mario Lemieux, the franchise's best player. But should there be more? No. Things are crowded enough on the North Shore. There are too many Steelers stars of equal Hall of Fame status to single out one, and the Pirates have exhausted their supply of iconic players who also spent their careers entirely with Pittsburgh. The statue population on the North Shore should be capped at four for now.

WHAT IS PITTSBURGH'S MOST ENDEARING SPORTS QUIRK?

There are some things surrounding sports that are uniquely Pittsburgh, and here are the top five.

5. ROONEY OWNERSHIP OF THE STEELERS

It's been that way since the franchise was founded in 1933 by Art Rooney Sr. He turned over control of the team to his son, Dan, in the late 1960s, and Dan handed off to his son, Art II, in 2002. That's 75 seasons with three people in charge, all of them named Rooney. Dan Rooney even lives in his father's old North Side house, which is within easy walking distance of Heinz Field. Another of Dan Rooney's sons, Dan Jr., is a scout for the Steelers and is credited with discovering running back Willie Parker, who played sparingly in college at North Carolina and wasn't drafted. At halftime at home games, Dan Rooney Sr. can usually be found in the press room, waiting his turn in line for a hot dog, or talking to old media friends. The NFL has become a multibillion dollar business, but the CEO in Pittsburgh is still approachable.

4. STEELERS TRAINING CAMP AT ST. VINCENT COLLEGE

A sleepy little Benedictine college in Latrobe, Pennsylvania, becomes an NFL focal point for six weeks every summer. (The Rolling Rock brewery, Latrobe's other famous industry, moved to New Jersey, but the city is apparently in no danger of losing the Steelers.) The Steelers have been coming to St. Vincent since the mid-1960s, and don't plan to move. A lot of teams have moved camp to their year-round training complexes, but the Steelers find value in the bonding experience that comes from cramming players into dorm rooms far from the temptations of the big city. Fans pack lunches and sit on the hillside, watching practices and collecting autographs from obscure free agents who will soon be back at day jobs.

3. VINTAGE BASEBALL USHERS

Have a question about Pirates' history? Ask your nearest PNC Park usher and prepare to get a detailed answer. Some medical school should do longevity studies on the baseball ushers, a lot of whom first worked games at Forbes Field, which closed during the 1970 season. It's rewarding part-time work for a lot of retirees, especially in the retro atmosphere of the riverfront ballpark. Pittsburgh's ushers have a union and actually went on strike several times at Three Rivers Stadium. The relationship with the Pirates was contentious then, with plenty of distrust on both sides. The relationship with the fans could be contentious too: Some of the ushers had a reputation for snarling at fans who didn't tip. Much of that has been ironed out at the new park and the ushers are fan-friendly. Ask one about Bill Mazeroski's World-Series-winning home run in 1960—there's a chance he was in Forbes Field that afternoon.

2. THE STEELERS' ONE HELMET LOGO

The Cleveland Browns have no emblem on their helmets. Everyone else has some sort of decoration on both sides, except the Steelers. They've been wearing their logo with the three diamond-shaped doo-dads (officially they're called hypercycloids) on the right side of their helmet since 1962. The logo came from the steel industry and the three hypercycloids represent the three elements used to make steel—yellow is coal, orange is ore, and blue is scrap. The Steelers weren't sure if the new logo would be permanent, so equipment manager Jack Hart was instructed to put just one on each helmet. After it caught on, the team decided it was distinctive to just have the logo on one side and kept it that way. Because of that, the Steelers helmet always has to be pictured facing right in order to be authentic. Do not believe urban legends, which hold that the Steelers didn't have enough stickers to equip all the helmets, or that an equipment helper didn't feel like doubling his work. The one-sided look is by design.

1. THE TERRIBLE TOWEL

Under orders from WTAE radio management, Myron Cope came up with this gimmick during the Steelers' 1975 playoff drive. (Lost trivia: The towel borrowed liberally from a babushka gimmick Bob Prince had invented for the Pirates earlier that year.) The Steelers were winning, the town was going crazy for anything black and gold, and the Terrible Towel was a sensation. Who knew it would endure more than 30 years later? Some of us thought the towel should have been retired after the Super Bowl era ended, but we were wrong. It's become a universal symbol for all things Pittsburgh. Hang one on your front porch in Nebraska and you'll immediately identify yourself to others as a Pittsburgh fan. Don't be surprised if a kindred spirit shows up with some Iron City some Sunday afternoon. The towels are all over the world, even proudly displayed by U.S. combat troops homesick in the Middle East. Cope, who was an exceptional magazine writer before he became a broadcast icon in Pittsburgh, has always joked that his proudest accomplishments will be dwarfed by his creation of the Terrible Towel. Considering its impact and its staying power for instant identification with Pittsburgh, maybe being known for the Terrible Towel isn't a bad thing at all.

WHAT ARE PITTSBURGH'S MOST ANNOYING SPORTS QUIRKS?

We've covered the endearing stuff, so let's get to the aggravating. These are the things the local sports world would never miss if they disappeared this afternoon.

5. PENGUINS FANS SELECTING A PLAYER TO BOO

This one has actually become almost obsolete. Penguins fans still delight in booing every time Jaromir Jagr touches the puck, but at least he plays for an opposing team. It used to be a tradition to single out one Penguins player—usually a defenseman—and let him have the same treatment. The Penguins certainly had enough bad players in the early years, but sometimes the designated target was a pretty decent player. Duane Rupp got the treatment, and so did Ron Stackhouse, a big defenseman who didn't hit much and rarely fought. Randy Carlyle was also getting the harassment in his last year with the Penguins, just a couple of years removed from the Norris Trophy. How irrational is this mass hysteria? Washington Capitals fans took to derisively whooping every time Larry Murphy touched the puck. Murphy was eventually traded and wound up with the Penguins. He was an integral part of the two Stanley Cup teams and was voted into the Hall of Fame. That proves the old saying, "He who whoops last...."

4. THE "HERE WE GO STEELERS" CHANT AT EVENTS THAT AREN'T STEELERS GAMES

This has become the local equivalent of the "bor-ing" chant that's popular in some places. If the Pirates or Penguins are playing a stinker, someone will start up the "Here We Go Steelers" chant. It doesn't even get irony points. It's just dumb, and further unfairly brands the region as a place where the two favorite sports are (1) football and (2) spring football.

3. HATING EVERYONE WHO LEAVES

This became especially prevalent when the Pirates started losing good players to free agency, but the fans who boo don't often read the small print. When pitcher John Smiley came back as a member of the Cincinnati Reds, fans booed when his name was announced. But Smiley never wanted to leave. He was traded by the Pirates, who were looking to cut payroll. Smiley, who wept when he was traded, continued to make his home in the Pittsburgh suburbs. Crying occurs on both sides: People were crying the night Jim Leyland managed his last game with the Pirates. When he came back after winning the 1997 World Series with the Florida Marlins, some fans booed.

The philosophy can be best summed up this way: "You left us? Okay, we never liked you anyway." It's part of the massive inferiority complex that afflicts Pittsburgh. According to a lot of fans, all network announcers are biased against Pittsburgh teams.

One of the few players who didn't get booed when he left as a free agent was first baseman Sid Bream. Yet Bream's demand for staying included a no-trade clause that would have put the Pirates at a disadvantage. No one seemed to notice that. Then again, no one ever said this practice made any sense.

2. SCAPEGOATING

Okay, Pittsburgh lost? Whose fault was it? It can't be that another quality team had a better day, or that a competitive game between equally matched teams was decided by one extra play. There has to be somebody to blame. So the final gun hadn't been sounded in Super Bowl XXX when it was decided that it was all quarterback Neil O'Donnell's fault. And it doesn't stop there.

In the 1992 National League playoffs against the Atlanta Braves, the Pirates didn't score enough runs, second baseman Jose Lind made a critical error, and right fielder Cecil Espy misplayed a ball—but it was all the fault of either reliever Stan Belinda, who gave up Francisco Cabrera's game-winning single, or left fielder Barry Bonds, whose throw to the plate was a bit late and a bit off-target. There were seven games in the series, and 9 innings in the finale, yet it all came down to one pitch and one throw. Why? Because it had to be somebody's fault. This trend is no doubt influenced by the volume (both in decibels and numbers) of talk shows and their need to fill hours and keep phones ringing.

1. RUMOR-MONGERING

This goes back at least to the 1970s, when the Pirates were still a big deal. A player would go on the disabled list and the word would circulate that the hamstring injury was just a cover-up. The "real" story was that a teammate had somehow stabbed or punched or otherwise attacked the poor victim. The stories almost always had racial overtones.

Later, the focus would shift to the Penguins, and finally the Steelers would get the full measure of the nonsense. In fact, the Steelers got the worst of it, because the Internet has become a much more effective way to spread the lies than the traditional system of barstool-to-barstool communication.

Things got so far out of hand that two Steelers went public with denials. Quarterback Kordell Stewart felt a need to stand before his teammates, then face reporters

293

and cameras to announce that he wasn't gay. Coach Bill Cowher opened one weekly news conference with a denial of marital difficulties. Most public relations experts advise clients not to address rumors, but the Steelers stories were so widespread that debunking the stories was deemed necessary. It's a shame the city has been such a fertile breeding ground for rumor-mongering.

WHO ARE FIVE GREAT VILLAINS OF PITTSBURGH SPORTS?

92 The mere mention of their names brings a negative reaction. They're the ones who have left an indelible and notorious mark on the Pittsburgh sports scene. Get ready to stand back if you dare to introduce these names in conversation:

5. ROGER MARINO

The Penguins were in financial trouble when undercapitalized owner Howard Baldwin found Marino, a Boston-based money man. Marino made a fortune in high-tech businesses, but liked the high profile that came with being in sports. He pumped $40 million into the Penguins on May 8,

1997. Just 17 months later, Marino had the Penguins filing for Chapter 11 bankruptcy, a process that put the franchise's Pittsburgh future in serious doubt. Marino's short tenure was stormy. He wound up in court with Mario Lemieux over contract payments, and he was shopping the franchise to other cities, most notably Kansas City. When the bankruptcy proceedings were over, Marino had about $40 million less in his personal fortune and a permanent place on Pittsburgh's enemies list.

4. DAVID VOLEK

When Volek's NHL career is remembered at all, it's recalled for his greatest moment—an overtime goal that knocked the Penguins out of the 1993 Stanley Cup playoffs. The Penguins had won two Stanley Cups and appeared to be getting better. They were fresh from a 119-point season that saw them finish first overall for the first time in franchise history. They had also breezed to a first-round victory over New Jersey and regarded the Islanders lightly. That was the problem.

Just 5:10 into overtime of game 7, Volek took a pass from Ray Ferraro and rifled a slapshot past Tom Barrasso. Mellon Arena fell so quiet, the Islanders could be heard celebrating the goal and the shocking end to the series. That goal ended the Penguins' hopes of a third consecutive Stanley Cup. It was the highlight for Volek, who played only 32 more NHL games before a herniated disc ended his career.

3. JACK TATUM AND GEORGE ATKINSON

These partners in the Oakland Raiders secondary are a single entry because they were part of the teams that had a fierce rivalry with the Steelers in the 1970s. Tatum and Atkinson were both vicious hitters who sometimes skirted the rulebook to intimidate opponents. Atkinson is best remembered for giving Lynn Swann a concussion in the 1975 AFC championship game, then clubbing Swann on the back of the helmet during the 1976 regular season and giving him another concussion. That led coach Chuck Noll to complain about a "criminal element" on the Raiders, which prompted Atkinson to file a $2 million defamation suit against Noll and the Steelers. Atkinson lost his case, but did succeed in inconveniencing Noll with courtroom obligations during training camp.

2. FRANCISCO CABRERA

This journeyman player has become an albatross to Pirates fans in the way that Bucky Dent is less-than-fondly recalled by fans of the Boston Red Sox. Cabrera had the game-winning hit for the Braves in game 7 of the 1992 National League playoffs, the Pirates' last good chance to get to the World Series. Cabrera had only batted eleven times in the regular season. He was called upon to pinch hit in the ninth inning and lined a 2–1 pitch from Stan Belinda to left field. His hit scored David Justice and Sid Bream and sent the Braves to the World Series. Cabrera's deed took on more significance when the Pirates then followed that playoff loss with 14 losing seasons.

1. AL DAVIS

Davis was such a perfect villain because he looked like one of Batman's foes—the Joker, the Riddler, the Raider.

Given the level of intensity between the Steelers and Raiders, Pittsburgh fans would have been inclined to dislike anyone associated with the Raiders. But Davis made it easy to ratchet it up to another level. The rivalry between the Raiders and Steelers was more than two football teams playing high-stakes games, it was a clash of cultures. Davis, who constantly dressed in the team's silver and black, represented the dark side, a team that operated in secrecy and provided a haven for the NFL's outcasts. The Steelers were as much of a mom-and-pop store as a multi-million dollar sports franchise could be. Yes, the Steelers had some players who would fit in with the Raiders (Greg Lloyd comes to mind), but basically the philosophical gulf between the two organizations was wide. The Steelers and Raiders haven't had serious issues in decades, and Davis is now old and frail. Yet he lingers as Pittsburgh enemy number one for what he meant in the 1970s.

WHAT WAS BETTER, "STUDIO WRESTLING" OR "BOWLING FOR DOLLARS?"

Is there a Pittsburgher anywhere who didn't at least sample these made-for-TV pseudo-sports shows?

Studio Wrestling was produced live in the studios of WPXI-TV (then known as WIIC) from the station's sign-on in 1957 through 1974. Bill Cardille hosted almost all of the program's run. *Bowling for Dollars* came from WTAE in the 1970s and was hosted by staffer Nick Perry, who was well known for his work on Saturday afternoon bowling competitions that were also on WTAE.

Studio Wrestling essentially served as an infomercial for the live cards that were held monthly at the Civic Arena and in various smaller towns throughout the region. The TV show allowed promoters to introduce characters and issues they hoped would motivate ticket sales for the live events. *Studio Wrestling* was initially an hour-long show, but was later stretched to 90 minutes. Cardille always welcomed viewers to "90 minutes of unorganized mayhem, featuring the greatest wrestlers in the world." The truth, of course, was that everything was carefully planned, and some of the wrestlers who appeared on the show held down day jobs as steelworkers (Johnny DeFazio) and police officers (Frank Holtz).

The station set up a regulation ring in one of its studios, then had about 100 people come in and watch the matches. Baseball Hall of Famer Pie Traynor did live commercials for the American Heating Company over the din, and Cardille ostensibly tried to keep order while pushing the storylines to promote the live matches. There were no locker rooms, so wrestlers killed time in the station lobby until it was time to appear. Station employees grew accustomed to having 240-pound Tony Marino wandering the halls in a full Batman outfit. They chatted amiably with Professor Turo Tanaka, a sneaky Japanese villain who was really Charlie Kelani, a jolly Hawaiian who had been a U.S. Marine Corps drill instructor before he started wrestling.

Studio Wrestling was systematically killed when the station became convinced that being known as the station with wrestling was undermining its reputation as a credible news source. The wrestlers finally got the boot in early 1974, chased to a UHF station for a brief time before the locally produced show gave way to a syndicated one. Cardille remained on staff at WPXI for another 20 years and still has a daily show on WJAS radio.

Bowling for Dollars was a chance for Pittsburgh-area bowlers to appear on TV and have a chance at winning a modest amount of money. Although many viewers probably never knew it, *Bowling for Dollars* was a franchise. The show used the same template in other cities and was localized solely by the host and contestants. The sliding-door set, format, and theme music were all provided by the same company that sold *Romper Room*. But the affable Perry made it a purely Pittsburgh experience by setting nervous participants at ease with a brief pre-roll interview. Here's a sample exchange:

"What do you like to do in your spare time, Chuck?"

"Bowling...TV...I work in my garden."

"What do you grow?"

"Oh, tomatoes...squash...peppers."

"Red peppers or green?"

Each participant brought friends and family, who waved shyly when they were acknowledged, The bowler would also add the inevitable greeting to "the guys down at work" and other friends and relatives who didn't make it to the studio. The jackpot went to anyone who rolled two strikes. Not many did with the pressure of lights and cameras, so they settled for a dollar a pin on their two attempts.

Bowling for Dollars had a good run in a Monday-through-Friday evening time slot, but eventually viewers grew tired of it and the show disappeared. Nick Perry, always introduced as "the man with all the money, the kingpin himself," would later become notorious as the mastermind of the "666" fix of the Pennsylvania lottery on April 24, 1980. He was convicted on a variety of charges and served two years in a state prison. Perry died in 2003.

So who's the winner of the hokiest sports show in town? *Studio Wrestling* takes the honors by a bodyslam. *Bowling for Dollars* had the emotional tug of everyday people trying to win a jackpot, but *Studio Wrestling* had Animals and Crushers and Killers all crammed into the same show, working under a carefully crafted blanket of deceit.

BURNING
QUESTIONS

WHY DOESN'T PITTSBURGH HAVE AN NBA TEAM?

 Pittsburgh has had Major League Baseball for more than a century, an NFL franchise since 1933, and has been part of the NHL for 40 years. But the city's involvement in pro basketball has been restricted to either start-up rival leagues or minor leagues that have flopped.

It started in 1961–1962, when Harlem Globetrotters impresario Abe Saperstein created the American Basketball League. The Pittsburgh Rens (short for Renaissance) were a charter member of the league, which included a Cleveland franchise owned by George Steinbrenner. The Rens finished second in the Eastern Division in 1961–1962, which turned out to be the only full season the ABL had. The league folded on December 31, 1962.

Basketball was back in Pittsburgh in 1967–1968, the same season that the Penguins joined the NHL. The Pittsburgh Pipers were an original member of the American Basketball Association, which distinguished its product with a red, white, and blue basketball. Maybe starting at the same time as the Penguins became an obstacle for the Pipers. Entertainment dollars were split in two directions, and the Pipers couldn't get a television station to carry any of their games.

That was too bad, because the Pipers were a pretty good show. The team was led by Connie Hawkins, a gifted player who had been banned from the NBA after he had been implicated in a college point-shaving scandal. Hawkins was one of the ABA's biggest stars and helped the Pipers win the league's first championship. There was a packed house at the Civic Arena for the title game, as the Pipers' growing success had finally established a fan base. But even as the team was celebrating the victory, its fate had been sealed. It wasn't publicly known, but owner Gabe Rubin had agreed to a deal that would move the franchise to Minneapolis.

The Pipers flopped in Minnesota, returning to Pittsburgh after one season. At that point, however, there were two major problems: Fans were understandably resentful that their team had been taken away, and the Pipers no longer had Hawkins. He won a court case that gained him admission to the NBA, and jumped to the established league to play for Phoenix.

In a move designed to inject some fresh air, in 1969 the Pipers were rechristened the Pioneers in a name-the-team contest. That didn't last long, though. Point Park College was using Pioneers for its sports teams, and threatened legal action to protect its trademark. The Pipers/Pioneers then adopted the name Condors, replacing their blue and orange colors with a bold red, orange, and white color scheme.

Despite aggressive marketing and some interesting players such as John Brisker and local favorite Mickey Davis, the Condors drew poorly and for all intents and purposes folded after two seasons. By March of 1972, the Condors were barnstorming, playing "home" games in Birmingham and Tucson. The team officially went of business in June of 1972 and the players were scattered in a dispersal draft.

A minor league attempt was next. The Continental Basketball Association (CBA) moved in with the Piranhas in 1994. The brand of basketball was decent, but selling a minor league franchise in a town accustomed to major league sports was tough. The team disbanded after one season. In recent years, another franchise, the XPlosion, has competed in a new ABA and the CBA with very little success in either league. They've drawn a few hundred fans to the 16,000-seat Mellon Arena.

Pittsburgh has never been on the NBA's hot list for either an expansion team or relocation of an existing franchise. With a shrinking market (the former number-nine television market is now number 23) and a mostly uninspiring pro hoops history, that disinterest is unlikely to change.

WHO ARE THE TOP-FIVE QUARTERBACKS PRODUCED BY WESTERN PENNSYLVANIA?

95 The region has become known as the cradle of quarterbacks and the reason is simple: High school football has always been important in western Pennsylvania, and it's always been played at a high level. The area has produced an abundance of good players, and it stands to reason there would be a good supply of quarterbacks among them. And who gets more notice in football than the quarterback?

This top five is so deep in talent that there's no room for George Blanda, a native of Youngwood, Pennsylvania, who spent 26 seasons in pro football and was elected to the Hall of Fame in 1981. Connellsville's Johnny Lujack failed to make the cut, too. He was the 1947 Heisman Trophy winner at Notre Dame. Willie Thrower from New Kensington gets honorable mention for being the first black quarterback in the modern NFL; he played for the Chicago Bears in 1953 after an exceptional career in Michigan State.

It's too soon to rate current Pittsburgh-bred NFL quarterbacks such as Mark Bulger, Bruce Gradkowski, and Charlie Batch because their careers are still in progress. Instead, let's take a look at this historical top five, all of whom have been inducted into the Pro Football Hall of Fame.

5. JOE NAMATH

Namath wasn't even sure he wanted to play college football when he came out of Beaver Falls High School. His first love was baseball, and six major league teams had made him offers. But his family wanted him to go to college, and Namath headed to the University of Alabama and coach Paul "Bear" Bryant, who would become one of the biggest influences on his life. Namath led Alabama to the national championship in 1964, then took New York by storm as the first-round draft pick of the American Football League's New York Jets. The flashy quarterback was also drafted by the NFL's St. Louis Cardinals, but he never would have been "Broadway Joe" in the Midwest. Nor would he have gotten a contract close to the $400,000 deal the Jets provided. Namath put the upstart American Football League on the map when his Jets defeated the Baltimore Colts in Super Bowl III, a result Namath had guaranteed in a poolside news conference. Chronic knee injuries were a constant problem, but Namath was voted into the Hall in 1985. For all of his celebrity in New York, Namath never forgot his roots. He chose his high school coach, Larry Bruno, as his presenter for the Hall of Fame induction.

4. JIM KELLY

Kelly grew up in East Brady, Pennsylvania, idolizing Terry Bradshaw, right down to wearing No. 12. Like Bradshaw, Kelly played in four Super Bowls, but his Buffalo Bills lost all of them. The championship was the only thing lacking in Kelly's career. He headed to the United States Football League out of college (Miami) and perfected the run-and-shoot offense. In two USFL seasons, Kelly threw for 9,842 yards and 83 touchdowns. He then went to Buffalo and took the Bills to the playoffs in eight of his 11 seasons. Kelly flourished in the Bills' no-huddle offense and was elected to the Hall of Fame in 2002.

3. DAN MARINO

You can't get any more purely Pittsburgh than Marino, who grew up in the city's Oakland section, just blocks from Central Catholic High School and the University of Pittsburgh, which were the first two steps in his career. Marino wasn't the most mobile quarterback, but he didn't have to be. His quick release and strong arm allowed him to make plays that other quarterbacks couldn't. A disappointing senior season at Pitt caused his draft stock to fall, but that worked out in the long run. He wound up with the Miami Dolphins, where he became the starter six weeks into his rookie season. Marino held that job through 1999, rewriting most of the NFL's passing records. He passed for 63,361 yards in his career, and his record of forty-eight touchdown passes in a season still stands. Marino was part of the Hall's 2005 class.

2. JOE MONTANA

There are people from the Monongahela Valley who remember this Ringgold High School product as an outstanding basketball player. Montana wasn't physically imposing, but no one was ever more cool in the heat of the game. The unflappable Montana engineered 31 fourth-quarter comebacks in his NFL career. After being third on Notre Dame's depth chart at the start of the 1977 season, he wound up leading the Fighting Irish to the national title. Montana won four Super Bowls with the San Francisco 49ers and was voted the Most Valuable Player in three of those games. He played his final two seasons with Kansas City and took the Chiefs to the playoffs in both years.

1. JOHNNY UNITAS

There are statues of Unitas in Louisville, where he played collegiately, and in Baltimore, where his leadership of the Colts made every Sunday a holiday. In Pittsburgh he's a monument to the bad judgment that afflicted the Steelers for too many years. They drafted Unitas in 1955, but cut him in training camp without letting him on the field during the exhibition season. Unitas went to the Colts, where he started from 1956 to 1972, leading Baltimore to NFL titles in 1958 and 1959 while winning the league MVP award in three seasons (1959, 1964, and 1967). He quarterbacked the Colts to a 23–17 win over the New York Giants in the legendary 1958 overtime championship game, which is given credit for establishing the NFL with television viewers across the country. Until that time, pro football had taken a back seat to college games in much of the nation. Unitas was hardly the most gifted athlete, but he was a natural leader who played in an era when quarterbacks were challenged to do their own play-calling. His record of touchdown passes in 47 consecutive games is considered as untouchable as Joe DiMaggio's 56-game hitting streak is in baseball.

Unitas is the best quarterback to play in the NFL, not just the best from western Pennsylvania.

WHO WAS THE BETTER PROFESSIONAL WRESTLER, BRUNO SAMMARTINO OR KURT ANGLE?

96 On most comparisons, you crack open the record book and look at career statistics. Professional wrestling doesn't operate that way since the outcomes are predetermined. Performers succeed because they've been chosen to succeed. But even that is not without merit—promoters make stars of the wrestlers they think will do the most box office business.

In this case, we have two Pittsburgh natives who rose to the top of their profession. Sammartino, who was born in 1936, survived World War II in his native Italy and came to America as a malnourished teenager. He began weightlifting to build his body. He was a construction worker who was asked to do some strongman stunts on Bob Prince's TV show. Wrestling promoter Rudy Miller spotted him and figured his raw strength and ethnicity could make him a hit in wrestling business. After a rocky start in 1959, Sammartino was chosen in 1963 to hold the title for the

World Wide Wrestling Federation, a Northeast-based promotion whose "worldwide" jurisdiction stretched as far west as Steubenville. Sammartino held the belt until January 1971, when, tired of being on the road, he semiretired from wrestling. Two years later he was back as champion to rescue the struggling WWWF. His second reign ended in 1977 and he wrestled sporadically after that.

Angle, born in 1968, was a multisport athlete at Mt. Lebanon High School, then went on to Clarion University, where he wrestled. After two NCAA Division I championships, he won a gold medal in freestyle at the 1996 Olympics. The old WWWF had by now evolved into the World Wrestling Federation, a global company that would soon become the only surviving wrestling company. WWF president Vince McMahon wanted Angle, but Angle declined his offer. Angle became a marketing rep for a company that sold ostrich meat, then tried sportscasting for Pittsburgh's WPGH-TV. Finally, he agreed to a three-year contract with the WWF in October of 1998 and began his training. He would rise to main-event status and hold the renamed WWE title on six different occasions. [

So we have two Pittsburgh wrestlers, two champions, from two distinctly different eras in the wrestling business. When Sammartino was champion, the monthly arena shows were the main source of revenue. In Angle's time, arena shows existed mostly to sell merchandise. The big money was in monthly pay-per-view events. The pace of the business changed, too, and the need for more product forced storylines to advance more rapidly. In Sammartino's time, secrecy about the nature of wrestling was paramount. Promoters tried to convince viewers they were seeing a real competition. Later, those standards were relaxed, McMahon renamed the product "sports entertainment," and fans appreciated the artistry while knowing they were watching a performance rather than contest.

Sammartino was clearly the biggest star in the WWWF from 1963 to 1981, a status Angle never attained, despite his title runs. Angle's wrestling style was much more athletic and he was a tremendous technical wrestler. Sammartino's time was more about stirring passions and slaying clumsy giants.

Sammartino has the edge on Angle in longevity at the top of his profession. Sammartino's drawing power helped the old WWWF stay in business, which indirectly provided Angle with a place to work decades later. Angle never had similar individual drawing power. But because the WWF expanded and television became more widespread, Angle is probably better known in a broader area.

Dave Meltzer, publisher of the *Wrestling Observer Newsletter*, has the best bottom line on the two: "In the end, this is comparing Babe Ruth with Barry Bonds. Barry Bonds may have been the overall better baseball player, but Babe Ruth is still going to be Babe Ruth. Angle was the better wrestler, but Sammartino is the more legendary wrestling figure."

WHICH WAS THE BETTER MELTDOWN, BILL COWHER'S STUFFED SHIRT OR LLOYD McCLENDON'S STOLEN BASE?

97

There's always emotion involved in sports, and it can reach a critical level when a team thinks it isn't getting a fair shake from officials.

Steelers coach Bill Cowher had a celebrated incident in a September 24, 1995, game against the Minnesota Vikings. Just before the first half ended, the Vikings lined up for a field goal and missed it. The teams were ready to leave the field, but there was a penalty flag. The Steelers were called for having 12 men on the field. The Vikings got 5 yards and made the field goal on the second chance.

Cowher was livid, maintaining the officials counted incorrectly and cost his team 3 points. While he was arguing, the upstairs coaching booth was providing evidence. They had an overhead Polaroid photo that clearly showed 11 Steelers on the field for the first attempt. The photo was faxed to the sideline and someone passed it to Cowher. Cowher rushed onto the field and tried to show the photo to referee Gordon McCarter as the officials were leaving the field. McCarter wasn't interested in listening, so Cowher shoved the photo in the referee's shirt pocket, then ran off the field. The call didn't change, and the NFL later fined Cowher $7,500.

Lloyd McClendon's moment came on June 26, 2001, in his first season as Pirates manager. McClendon was convinced the umpires didn't take the last-place Pirates seriously. He thought first-base umpire Rick Reed missed two calls; the second was a close play involving Jason Kendall. McClendon went out to argue the call and became more enraged as the discussion continued. After he was ejected, he walked over, uprooted first base, and stormed off the field with the bag under his arm. He carried it into the dugout, throwing down the base as he disappeared down the tunnel to the clubhouse.

The fans loved it, roaring approval as McClendon stomped off. The umpires instructed the grounds crew to install a new base. Pirates left fielder Brian Giles retrieved the original base and kept it in a vacant locker next to his, a shrine to McClendon's spirited protest. After the game, McClendon told reporters, "(Reed) wasn't seeing it. I figured I might as well take it with me."

The incident eventually became something of an albatross

for McClendon because umpires don't like to be embarrassed. The Pirates included footage of the episode in a highlights package shown on the scoreboard before every game. McClendon eventually asked the team to delete the scene. He was fined an undisclosed amount by the commissioner's office.

Which incident gets the nod? Cowher had a point, but he violated a basic rule: Never touch an official. Besides, it took him two attempts to get the photo in McCarter's pocket. McClendon wins this one for originality and style points. Everyone probably expected him to throw the base. Walking off with it was a better way to make his point.

WHAT WAS WESTERN PENNSYLVANIA'S GREATEST HIGH SCHOOL BASKETBALL TEAM?

Yes, the region is famous for its Friday night football in the fall, but there have been some legendary basketball teams, too. The quality of play has declined with the population drop, however, which meant the 2007 Schenley state championship team was given high praise when it was mentioned for the all-time western Pennsylvania top ten.

For this one, we leaned on the expertise of veteran hoops watchers Steve Hecht, Rich Emert, Mike White, and the legendary "Deuce" Skurcenski. They also had considerable input from the guys who hang around the *Pittsburgh Post-Gazette*'s sports department and never lack opinions.

Here's how the consensus stacked up with these championship teams.

5. SCHENLEY, 1966

This squad was led by Kenny Durrett, who went on to a stellar college career at LaSalle. Durrett is considered by many the finest player in Philadelphia's formidable college basketball history. He was the fourth player chosen in the 1971 NBA draft, but a knee injury prevented him from having much of a pro career.

4. FIFTH AVENUE, 1976

What a way to go. Fifth Avenue High School closed that summer and the basketball team delivered one last state championship. Sam Clancy, a 6-foot, 6-inch forward, led the squad. Clancy was an accomplished enough athlete to last 11 seasons in professional football after a basketball career up the street at the University of Pittsburgh. David

"Puffy" Kennedy and Bill Clarke helped make this team special.

3. SCHENLEY, 1971

The stars here were Maurice Lucas, Rickey Coleman, and Jeep Kelley. Lucas went on to a 14-year NBA career that saw him score more than 14,000 points and help the Portland Trail Blazers to a championship. This team sent four players (Tom Thornton was the other) to major Division I college programs.

2. MIDLAND, 1965

This was arguably the region's best team in terms of pure talent. Norm Van Lier and Simmie Hill were the leaders. Van Lier was just 6 feet and 1 inch, but played stifling defense and had a passion for the game. He had a long NBA career with the Chicago Bulls. Hill, a gifted 6-foot, 7-inch forward, had the ability to be just as good in the pros, but could never quite get his act together. He was a first-round choice in the ABA and a second-round pick in the NBA draft. Hill put in time with a number of teams in several pro leagues. The Midland squad was coached by Hank Kuzma. The Leopards had a perfect 28–0 season.

1. AMBRIDGE, 1967

The Midland vs. Ambridge debate is the local version of the old "Willie, Mickey, or the Duke" debate about center fielders in New York in the 1950s. Ambridge had a good nucleus of talent, and everything came together when coach Chuck DeVenzio came to Ambridge from Springdale and brought his point-guard son Dick with him. Dick DeVenzio averaged 31 points per game, Dennis Wuycik contributed size and power, and Frank Kaufmann, Walt Ostrowski, and Phil DePasquale rounded out the squad perfectly. Like the 1965 Midland team, the 1967 Bridgers went undefeated and had a lopsided win in the state championship game. This team created such a mania for basketball that Ambridge set up a closed circuit TV system to accommodate the fans who couldn't fit into the tiny gym. The elder DeVenzio was a coach right out of central casting, a gruff, gravel-voiced man who demanded his team play the game the right way. Dick DeVenzio was possessed, regularly practicing his game for hours in the summer. The coach's son was a coach on the floor during games. Under the dual DeVenzio influence, this was the perfect team.

WHO WERE THE GREATEST INFLUENCES ON PITT ATHLETICS?

99

The athletic programs at Pitt have been up and down over the years, often depending on the level of attention they get from the administration. Most of Pitt's sports programs were brought up to speed in the 1970s, when the university made athletics a bigger priority. There has been another renaissance in recent years with new facilities for both the football and basketball programs.

Here's a look at the five most important names in Pitt sports.

5. EARLY 1970s BOOSTERS

Several hard-core Pitt sports supporters were fed up with the moribund football program and decided to do something about it. They raised money, put the wheels in motion to go after Johnny Majors, and wound up turning around Pitt football. The administration was mostly an innocent bystander while this was happening, although some members were happy to jump in the celebratory pictures after the 1976 national championship.

4. BEN HOWLAND

Ambitious and driven, Howland took over a basketball program in 1999 that had sagged under Ralph Willard's leadership. Howland installed a system of tight defense and got the players to buy into it, amazing in an era when so much of basketball is about making spectacular individual plays. Howland worked through a 13–15 debut season, weeded out dissidents, then made the NIT in his second season. That was followed by two appearances in the NCAA Sweet Sixteen. The ambition that brought Howland to Pitt from Northern Arizona flared again, and he was gone to his dream job with UCLA. The haste of his departure soured some on what he accomplished, but he got the program on solid footing and left behind a capable successor in Jamie Dixon. Thanks to Howland, Pitt fans now expect an NCAA Tournament bid.

3. TONY DORSETT

The Hopewell High School running back had his choice of offers when he graduated in 1972, yet he chose Pitt, which was coming off a 1–10 season. Dorsett gave in to the persuasion of new head coach Johnny Majors and became the signature recruit for the new football program. He was a star as a freshman and by the time he left, he set an NCAA record with 6,082 career rushing yards. Dorsett also won the Heisman Trophy, Maxwell Award, and Walter Camp Award. His presence gave the program instant credibility and helped establish a recruiting base.

2. STEVE PEDERSON

Controversial for sure, but Pederson shook up the campus in a good way when he took over as athletic director in 1996. He was a visionary who orchestrated the demolition of ancient Pitt Stadium and used that land to build a state-of-the-art Petersen Events Center. Under Pederson's watch, the Panthers' football program partnered with the Steelers on a training and practice complex on the South Side. Pitt also agreed to take its home football games off campus and rent Heinz Field from the Steelers. With Pederson in charge, the football program made three straight bowl trips. He rubbed some people the wrong way by insisting on "Pittsburgh" over "Pitt" in media references to the school, but Pederson was good for the Panthers, whatever they were called.

1. JOHNNY MAJORS

He came to Pitt from Northern Iowa, but he was a southern gentleman who came to the football program preaching the virtues of pride and enthusiasm. Relaxed NCAA regulations let him bring in overwhelming numbers of players. The staff sorted through them all, had a good year, and made a trip to the new Fiesta Bowl in Majors's first season. They earned a bowl game in three of his four years, which kicked off a streak of ten bowl appearances in 11 years. Majors was evangelistic in spreading the word about Pitt football and was a dynamic recruiter. Pitt was 33–13 in his four seasons and capped that run with an undefeated season and national championship in 1976.

Then Majors's alma mater, Tennessee, came calling, and he left. With the football program in desperate straits in the 1990s, Pitt brought Majors for an encore after he'd been deposed from his job at Tennessee. It didn't work, and he left after going 12–32 in four seasons. Majors then took an administrative job with Pitt and remains associated with the university. It says something about his accomplishments in the 1970s that his record was not tarnished a bit by the ill-fated return in the 1990s. Johnny Majors put Pitt football on the map, and no one would forget that.

BUZZER
BEATER

IS THERE ANYTHING SPORTS-RELATED THAT'S BETTER IN CLEVELAND THAN PITTSBURGH?

100 Even though Pittsburgh-based H. J. Heinz has been making condiments since 1869, Cleveland has a brown mustard that's the perfect complement to a well-grilled all-beef stadium hot dog (www.stadiummustard.com). The product has even made its way to Pittsburgh supermarket shelves.

But other than that? Don't be silly.

INDEX
By Subject

THE BEST PITTSBURGH SPORTS ARGUMENTS

347

349

351

ACKNOWLEDGMENTS

Thanks to the following for their assistance: Lisa Lynch, Steve Hecht, Bob Carroll, Jeff Gerson, Mike White, Rich Emert, Neil Rudel, Bob Jinkerson, Cara Taback, Dave Meltzer, Chuck Moody, Joe Taylor, Tim DeBacco, John Barbero, Nat Loubet, Dennis Natale, Helen King, David Stout, Elizabeth Hensley, and DC Lynch.

ABOUT THE AUTHOR

John Mehno began covering Pittsburgh sports in 1974 for *Steel City Sports*, a weekly publication that turned into *Score! Pittsburgh* before it closed in 1977. Since then, he's handled thousands of assignments for the Associated Press, and his columns and game coverage appear regularly in a number of newspapers, including the *Beaver County Times, Altoona Mirror*, and *Pittsburgh Sports Report*. His byline has appeared in *USA Today, Washington Post, Chicago Sun-Times*, and *Dallas Morning News.* He served as a baseball correspondent for *The Sporting News* for thirteen years and was a frequent guest host of "Drive Time Sports" on WJAS-AM in Pittsburgh. He has written two other books, *The Chronicle of Baseball* (Carlton, 2000, updated and revised in 2005) and *The Best Book of Football Facts and Stats* (Carlton, 2003).